EXPLORIN
FINANCIAL UNIVERSE

EXPLORING THE FINANCIAL UNIVERSE

The Role of the
Sun and Planets in the
World of Finance

Christeen H. Skinner

Ibis Press
Lake Worth, FL

Published in 2016 by Ibis Press
A division of Nicolas-Hays, Inc.
P. O. Box 540206
Lake Worth, FL 33454-0206
www.ibispress.net

Distributed to the trade by
Red Wheel/Weiser, LLC
65 Parker St. • Ste. 7
Newburyport, MA 01950
www.redwheelweiser.com

ISBN 978-0-89254-218-5
Ebook: ISBN 978-0-89254-632-9

Library of Congress Cataloging-in-Publication Data
Names: Skinner, Christeen, author.
Title: Exploring the financial universe : the role of the sun and planets in
the world of finance / Christeen H. Skinner.
Description: 1st [edition]. | Lake Worth, FL : Ibis Press an imprint of
Nicolas-Hays, Inc, 2016. | Includes bibliographical references and index.
Identifiers: LCCN 2016033997 (print) | LCCN 2016034568 (ebook) |
ISBN 9780892542185 (alk. paper) | ISBN 9780892546329 ()
Subjects: LCSH: Astrology and business. | Astrology and personal finance. |
Business--Miscellanea. | Finance, personal--Miscellanea.
Classification: LCC BF1729.B8 S55 2016 (print) | LCC BF1729.B8 (ebook) |
DDC 133.5/8332--dc23
LC record available at https://lccn.loc.gov/2016033997

Book design and production by Studio 31
www.studio31.com

[MV]

Printed in the United States of America

Contents

Introduction

I am hesitant to describe myself as a financial astrologer. For a start, I do not have recognized qualifications in financial management. I am not licensed by the Financial Services Authority here in the UK and cannot give financial advice. Even so, in my work as an astrologer I have drifted into the world of business and finance and have a client base of market-traders, investors, chief executive officers, and entrepreneurs.

Through working with these people I have learned to understand market rhythms and the links between these and planetary cycles. For investors and designers I have become a future-caster, determining trends well ahead of time. CEOs have asked opinions on everything from share price movement to forecasting periods of potential cash flow difficulty, while entrepreneurs have asked about timing, actual location, and general management.

In response to their regular inquiries, I began to write to these clients on a Sunday evening outlining planetary conditions for the week ahead. Some forwarded this letter to friends and colleagues. This developed into a more impersonal newsletter service in 2001. By 2008 it had morphed into the *Full Moon Financial Universe* letter which will soon reach its hundredth issue.

Following requests from readers of the newsletter, in 2014, I offered two short financial astrology courses that took the form of a series of six Sunday webinars. Along the way it was suggested that I should collate the ideas presented and turn these into a book. This is that book. It is, as its title suggests, an exploration.

Exploring the Financial Universe begins by considering solar activity and the influence of solar rhythms on trading. That chapter is followed by a review of the astrology of the Global Financial Crisis that was centered on 2008 but which is, I think, as yet unfinished. My reasoning is based on a study of stock market crashes of the 20th century as shown in Chapter Three. As will be seen, there are similar formations in the years ahead and high probability of further financial debacle as Pluto travels through Capricorn.

Many people are intrigued by the possibility of making spectacular financial gain through using astrological techniques. In Chapter Four, examples of days of major gains and major losses are given. There does indeed seem to be correlation with planetary activity. The chapter concludes with a list of aspects and planet positions to look out for. This list should be of value to both investors and traders.

Chapter Five considers the links between planet positions and recessions, the construction and land price cycles, and the real estate market.

Foreign exchange is given attention in Chapter Six which covers the Euro, the US dollar, and a brief look at one of the newest currencies, Bitcoin. Chapter Seven covers the links between planetary cycles and a few commodities: including gold, silver, platinum, cotton, corn, and sugar.

Chapter Eight covers Time and Price and considers the links between actual share price and planet positions. As with foreign exchange and commodities, I hope to develop this chapter into a book of its own. For now, examples used include Google, Walmart, and General Motors.

Chapter Nine, entitled "Your Own Chart" would have been excluded from this work, were it not for the interest shown by readers of the Full Moon letter who take the time to email, responding to comments made about personal finance. In time I suspect that this chapter too will become a book in its own right. For now, it includes various astrological techniques which have served me well in my work.

The penultimate chapter of this work offer first an overview of the coming years, followed by a more detailed look at 2018–2020 with key dates.

Exploring the Financial Universe will be followed by a *Beginner's Guide to the Financial Universe*, to be published by Ibis Press early in 2017.

CHRISTEEN SKINNER
March 2016

CHAPTER ONE

SOLAR ACTIVITY, PLANET CYCLES, AND THE WORLD OF FINANCE

It is now several hundred years since astronomy and astrology were taught as one subject. The divergence of the two disciplines is unfortunate and perhaps particularly so for the astro-trader, for whom understanding of solar conditions and planetary cycles offers unique perspective. Exploration of the financial universe must start with a review of recent solar activity. In forecasting trends, an appreciation of the solar conditions on which mankind depends is imperative.

It is convenient for us to think of our Sun as a ball of fire but it is, in fact, a ball of gas which appears in the sky as a circle—an optical illusion. However, its shape and size fluctuate, with solar flares and bursts of energy causing its size and shape to be ever-changing. The electromagnetic emissions, carried through the solar winds, take the form of radio, x-ray, and gamma waves which can be measured. The strength of these waves has considerable effect on life in all forms, on terrestrial weather system and, with the development of global communication systems (satellites etc), the computerized information highway on which traders have come to rely.

In particular, and as one cycle—the sunspot cycle—ebbs and flows, so does the number of geomagnetic occurrences in which there is a temporary disturbance of the Earth's magnetosphere caused by a solar wind shock wave interacting with the Earth's magnetic field. These events have the potential to disrupt satellite communication systems and, as they are as yet unpredictable, could yet cause mayhem at many levels.

In the case of the latter, consider this: at 07.04 EST on May 13, 1921 a solar magnetic storm was the cause of signal and switching system failure on the New York Central Railroad below 125th Street. The same storm affected telephone, telegraph, and cable traffic across Europe.

Can you imagine the economic effect of the widespread disruption of communications should a similar event occur today?

A rather different, but no less powerful solar action: this time a Coronal Mass Ejection on March 9, 1989, resulted in a severe geomagnetic storm bringing short wave radio interference that prompted some US military experts to think that the Soviets were attacking. This solar eruption lasted for some time and, at 2:44am on March 13, 1989, Hydro-Quebec's power grid was adversely affected: leading to a nine hour shut down—once again with major economic consequences. In August of that same year, another storm produced a halt to trading on the Toronto stock market; their computer systems were affected.

Helioseismologists, who study solar storms, know far more now than they did even half a century ago. Yet even today it is hard to predict solar activity and then have in place systems to prevent serious harm.

The big question is: "What causes solar output to vary?" The likely candidates may be the planets.

We know that the planets are held in orbit by their gravitational relationship with the Sun. The interconnection between each planet and the Sun varies according to the position and size of the planet involved. It may be that the positions of the planets collectively impacts activity on and in the Sun itself, though of course, the truth may be far more complex—and exciting. (Read Gregory Sams' fascinating book *Sun of gOd* for thoughts on our sun's consciousness.)

There are times when several planets are closely grouped. The pull or gravitational forces they each exert on our special star creates intense activity; manifesting as swirls or sunspots and coronal holes on its surface. Moreover, the presence of two of the planet "gas giants" (Jupiter, Saturn, Uranus, Neptune) on one side of the Sun is enough to pull the Sun toward it, resulting in spectacular eruptions of energy on that side of the Sun. In 2020, Jupiter and Saturn are joined by Pluto on one side of the Sun, and are joined for some days in early 2021, by Mercury, Venus, and Mars. The potential for significant solar activity is clearly signalled.

Dr Theodor Landscheit has worked in the field of solar

science for many years. His book *Sun-Earth-Man* published by the Urania Trust in 1987 is a classic. Since then Dr Landscheit and others have continued to study the effect of the gravitational pull of the planets on the Sun. They now have an impressive list of accurate forecasts to their credit. You can find out more at *www. john-daly.com/solar/solar.htm.*

Given the planet pictures for 2020 and 2021, it is reasonable to forecast extraordinary activity with probable consequences in the world of finance. These are explored in the concluding chapters of this book.

While focus on the early years of the next decade is understandable given the extraordinary line-up of planets, we should also take note of the longer cycles associated with solar activity.

100 and 510 YEAR CYCLES DROUGHT CYCLES:
THE WHEELER CYCLE

A drought cycle was determined by Professor Raymond Wheeler of the University of Kansas. He found an average cycle length of approximately 100 years (varies between 70 and 120 years) which he later thought to be part of a much longer, perhaps 510-year cycle.

This 510-year cycle compares favorably with the Neptune-Pluto cycle where the two planets appear aligned every 492 years. Within each Neptune-Pluto conjunction-to-conjunction cycle of 492 years, there are five shorter declination cycles of varying length but whose average is 100 years. Certainly it is worth exploring the two Neptune-Pluto cycles against Wheeler's two cycles.

As he suggested, the 500-year cycle coincides with marked shift of economic activity from the East to West hemisphere and back again. The most recent Neptune-Pluto conjunction took place at the end of the 19th century and already it is possible to see that the balance of trade is moving Eastward, just as the earlier one which coincided with Columbus' discovery of the Americas, witnessed emphasis on Western trade.

Though this longer cycle is not of obvious interest to today's market traders, the phase of the shorter 100-year cycles is of use—particularly to those trading soft commodities. Understanding of these cycles is of value in forecasting years of probable plenty (and therefore low prices) and leaner years when prices are likely to rise.

Wheeler's work indicated that the 100-year cycle could be divided into four distinct phases: "Cold-Dry," followed by "Warm-Wet," which is in turn followed by "Warm-Dry," with the final phase being "Cold-Wet." His study traced at least 78 major climate changes since 2500 BC with international wars occurring mostly during the warm periods and civil ones during colder periods.

While Wheeler's average 100-year cycle can be divided into four distinct phases, they are not of equal length. The present Warm-Dry period began in the late 1990s and should last through to the early 2020s but might extend for longer. It is not uncommon for police states to emerge during Warm-Dry periods. The emergence of ISIS or Daesh suggests that we are still within a Warm-Dry period. These periods have also coincided with decline in business confidence and a collapse of economic systems. The global financial crisis of 2008 fits with this phase. It should also be noted that as the Warm-Dry phase is clearly still operative, another collapse in business confidence and economic calamity could yet occur before the phase draws to its end.

The next phase, Cold-Wet begins with temperatures cooling and increased rainfall. This should coincide with improvement in crop production and general revival. Though it is not possible to give clear forecast as to when this next phase might begin, it is

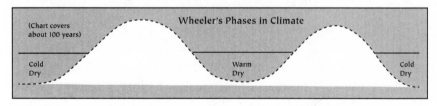

Data source: Raymond H. Wheeler (1943)
The Effect of Climate on Human Behavior in History.
In: *Transactions of the Kansas Academy of Science*, Vol. 46.

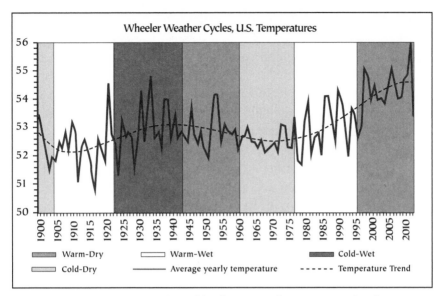

Data source: NOAA, http://cyclesresearchinstitute.org/cycles-research-weather/weather-wheeler.shtml • nowandfutures.com

likely to be post the next solar minima and possibly from 2022.

A key point of Professor Wheeler's research was that 90% of leaders of nations whom history now records as being "good" or even "great" led during the phase which he called "cold-dry." They presided over periods when chaos, as characterised by social unrest, declined. If Wheeler is correct, then we have some time to wait before those leaders are in a position to lead. The cold dry phase could be as much as six or seven decades away. Assuming those new leaders to be aged 40 + , then their births will not be recorded for another 20–30 years. It seems likely that these individuals will be born with Pluto in the sign of Aries. The sub-personality features associated with Pluto in Aries will include powerful Tarzan-figures comfortable with wielding power.

THE 190-YEAR CYCLE

The Sun and its system rotate in counter-clockwise motion around a central point known as the Barycenter: the center of mass of the solar system. Just as the Sun exerts a gravitational pull on the planets, the planets exert a pull on the Sun which orbits the Bary-center in a counter-clockwise direction. However, on seven occasions in the last four thousand years (approximately every 190 years) the combined position of the great planets Jupiter, Saturn, Uranus and Neptune have created a pull that has resulted in the Sun rotating clockwise relative to the solar system Barycenter. At these times, the Sun is said to be retrograde as happened in 1632, again between 1810 and 1812 and through 1989 and 1990.

Meteorological studies show that the period post-solar-retrograde (lasting up to 30 years) brings disturbed weather patterns. These then result in shorter growing seasons and, inevitably, higher food costs.

We are still in one of these post-solar retrograde periods and evidence of disturbed weather patterns is all around. Actually, given present solar data, it may be that the 30-year period post the most recent retrograde (1990) will last far longer. This could pose a real economic challenge with food prices rising as a direct consequence of decreased crop production.

Understanding of this approximately 190-year cycle enabled astro-economists to suggest that from 1990 onward there might be mass migration of peoples as people sought better conditions under which they could sustain themselves. It was always likely that the period 1990–2020 would be a time of extraordinary social and subsequent political and economic upheaval as has now proved to be the case.

While presently much attention is given to the fact that many are seeking refuge from war or migrating to find work, it is also true that solar activity has been, though perhaps unconsciously, an important driver in prompting many people to seek better living conditions. As solar activity stabilizes, the numbers of people on the move should decrease.

SUN SPOTS

Scientists track another solar cycle by counting sunspots—cool planet-sized areas on the Sun where intense magnetic loops poke through the star's visible surface. The sunspot cycle has an average length of 11.2 years. This cycle can, in fact, be as short as 9.4 years and as long as a little over 14 years. Numbering of solar cycles began in the 19th century making the present sunspot cycle number 24. The most recent minima (little to no sign of sunspots) occurred in 2008. If "on cue" at an average length of 11.2 years, then the next solar minimum should be recorded in 2019. There are reasons to think that the present cycle might last a little longer however:

In 2009 there was a period of over 200 days when no sunspot activity was recorded. In 2010 the numbers were not particularly high. By 2015 (when maxima was expected, numbers were still relatively low compared to the cycle maxima of 2000. Indeed, this present cycle has greatest similarity with Cycle 14 at the beginning of the last century when the recorded number of sunspots was also low.

The researcher, Arthur Schuster, determined that good wine years in Germany corresponded with years of minimum sun spots—a fact that may be of interest to investors and wine connoisseurs alike.

Another study (Tchijevsky 1926) suggested that wars, revolutions and mass movements with their resulting political, social and economic consequences coincided with high levels of sun spot activity.

Sunspots give off solar flares which in turn increase negative ionization on earth—which might explain increased excitability and activity during solar maxima. (Tchijevsky noted that particularly severe battles regularly followed a solar flare during the sunspot peak period of 1916–17.)

By contrast, the astro-economist David Williams' studies in the 1950s showed that the US had been engaged in either war or experienced depression during alternate periods of *low* sunspot activity. These findings appear to contradict Tchijevsky. However, it might simply be that when sunspots are at either minima or maxima there is extreme behavior on Earth.

There was a sunspot peak of 1969. A year earlier, and as the number of sunspots increased, there were riots across the United States, in Pakistan and in Malaysia.

A little over 11 years later (the average length of a sunspot cycle), in the early 1980s peak solar activity coincided with riots in Miami (May 1980), in London (April 1981), severe fighting in the Lebanon (July 1981), and the Israeli march into that country in June 1982. Each of these events coincided with significant solar activity.

It is interesting to also note that volcanic eruptions and earth disturbances (earthquakes) have tended to occur at times of peak solar activity. Where these coincide with key phases in the lunar cycle and, in particular, the Moon's relative position to Earth, the effect is magnified.

Solar maximum was reached in 1980, 1990, and 2000/2001. In 1980, Mt Helen's erupted. In 1989, there was a large earthquake affecting San Francisco, followed a year alter by a huge earthquake in Iran that killed 40,000. Then in 1991, Mounts Penatubo, Popo-catpetyl and Colima erupted. On each of these occasions the Moon was either at perigee or apogee: a fact that may be crucial to the level of chaos and destruction caused.

As mentioned above, 11.2 years is actually the *average* length of the sun-spot cycle: at times this cycle has been as short as 9.4 years and, on occasion, has lasted almost 14 years. This variability renders forecasting extremely difficult as, if we do not understand what prompts the increase and later decline in activity, we cannot make reliable and timely forecasts of related social unrest.

Yet, we can be clear that sunspots are electromagnetic disturbances produced by external charges on the sun's inner core. Those "external charges" may be directly linked to the position of the four planets: Jupiter, Saturn, Uranus and Neptune.

Jupiter is the largest of the known bodies orbiting the Sun. It is huge: greater than the sum of all the other known planets. At certain times in its orbit, Jupiter can "draw the Sun" out— apparently causing the Sun to go into a period of frenetic solar activity. When Jupiter is joined by Saturn, Uranus or Neptune, then the effect is even greater.

Jupiter's orbit is actually 11.88 years. During that time-frame it will form conjunctions and oppositions with Saturn, Uranus and Neptune though rarely two of these planets within the same year. The alignment in 1990—when Jupiter was at one side of the Sun while Saturn, Uranus and Neptune were on the other side—was unusual. Jupiter's position may have been yet another factor in the number of earth disasters that took place within months of Jupiter's opposition to the Sun.

Whereas Jupiter and Uranus form a conjunction every 14 years and Jupiter and Neptune every 13 years, Jupiter and Saturn form conjunctions every 20 years. As we shall see, this offers an important cyclical rhythm.

The conjunctions of Jupiter and Saturn never happen in exactly the same zodiacal area yet form a pattern over a number of years. In a later chapter will study this pattern with particular reference to the upcoming alignment in 2020.

The position of Jupiter and Saturn, by sign—and by default their relationship to the Sun's position in the zodiac—seems to play a key role in weather patterns. When these two planets align with the solar apex (the line of the Sun's advance), major droughts have been recorded. Actually, even Jupiter alone crossing the solar apex has been known to bring major drought—the most recent being in 2007 which saw a food crisis in some parts of the world.

That year marked a solar minimum when few sunspots meant reduced rain. In Australia this was keenly felt. The Murray River was almost dry in some parts. Jupiter was then traveling through the sign of Capricorn: the sign to which it returns in 2019. This could yet prove to be another year of drought. Worryingly, Saturn, though some degrees distant from Jupiter, will be on the same side of the Sun. Saturn moves much slower than Jupiter. Its position in 2019 draws attention to the Solar Apex (that point in the Galaxy to which our Sun and its attendant system appear to be traveling). This could mean that the drought extends into 2020. Prolonged drought would clearly be bad news for farmers. Following poor harvest, food prices could rise dramatically.

If these years do indeed bring a period of solar minimum, this promises to be a period of high drama at every level: from food shortage to wars and economic chaos.

Though it is not possible to say for certain that solar minimum will be reached in 2019, it does now seem likely that solar maximum was reached early in 2014. With the number of

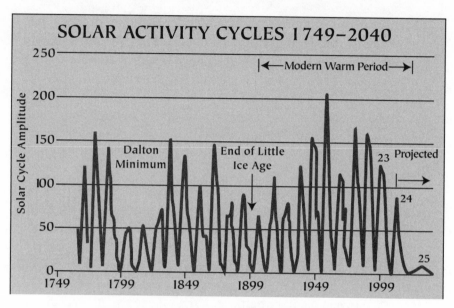

Data source: Solar Activity Cycles, David Rose,
The Mail on Sunday, www.dailymail.co.uk.

sunspots declining, unless there is an unusual spike of activity, then Cycle 24 will draw to a close in 2018–19. Note that the "typical" number of spotless (minima) days is 486 **consecutive** days. The minima period in Cycle 24 held for much longer than expected. Solar maximum brought readings of approximately 100 sunspots in a day when in the past double that number has been reached. The Sun therefore should be considered to be "quiet."

If Cycle 25 begins in 2019 and is of short duration as conjectured by some solar scientists, then this cycle could peak as early as 2022. This was proposed at the Royal Astronomical Society's National Association Meeting in 2015 by the Russian scientist Zharkova. If correct, then, just as solar minimum in 2019 should bring dramatic events, so too might 2022 or 2023 (minimum). If the 11-year cycle is operative however, then maximum would be reached a little later in 2025.

The forecasts for Cycles 25 and 26 do not bode well. These forecasts suggest continuing low levels of solar activity perhaps replicating earlier cycles that led to periods now dubbed the Dalton and Maunder minimums.

It may be that far from there being a rise in global temperatures as is feared by many, that the opposite will be the case and that a much colder and possibly hostile environment awaits. If this is the case—and certainly the increase in ice in the Antarctic suggests that this might be so, then by the next sunspot cycle maximum (2022–25), present-day refugees could yet choose to return to their native lands.

What is clear is that an increase in human activity coincides with solar maximum, even when that maximum is not as great as those of earlier cycles. This might be explained by the fact that as sunspot activity increases so too does magnetic disturbance.

It is well known that many living organisms contain magnetic materials (dolphins being the one with which we are most familiar). Magnetic material is also found in water and in certain bacteria. Perhaps significantly such material has not yet been found *in* humans though this force field is recognized by kinesiologists. It is entirely possible that changes in the magnetic energies released on solar winds do indeed have effect on all living material, and that the effect this has on human behavior results in highly-charged responses giving rise to social events of some magnitude.

Most people would surely agree that as the number of sunspots increased from 2010 to early 2014 when Cycle 24 is said to have peaked, so too have the number of major political events. Though certainly we can see the influence of the Uranus-Pluto square (2010–15) in everything from the Arab Spring to the spread of ISIS, an increase in sunspot activity may well have been another—and important—factor in the highly-charged responses and deviant behavior experienced in many parts of the world.

SUNSPOT DOUBLE CYCLE

Correlation between solar activity and movement at the very center of the Earth can be found when the double cycle of sunspot activity is taken into account. The double cycle seems rather more regular than the averaged 11.2 year single cycle. The double cycle has an average of approximately 22.2 years and does not vary as much as the single cycle, which as can vary between a little over nine and 14 years.

Though sunspots appear randomly on the Sun's surface they do follow a rhythm. The first sunspots of a new cycle appear in the upper hemisphere of the Sun's surface. As they increase, they appear to move down over the Sun's equator to the lower hemisphere where, a little over half-way down and after approximately 11.2 years, they start to move back up over the Sun's surface. A single cycle then moves in one direction and the following in the opposite direction.

It is the "double cycle"—describing the total cycle between sunspots forming in the northern hemisphere of the sun, gradually crossing its equator and moving to the southern hemisphere, then returning to the northern hemisphere—that may have greatest influence on the Earth's core. Interestingly it is said that we know more about the Sun's inner core than we do that of the Earth's. What is known is that at the very center of the Earth, currents create a dynamo effect that in turn generates the Earth's magnetic field that protects life in all forms from annihilation by solar flares.

In 1993 and 2003 two earthquakes occurred in the Pacific Ocean and were just half a mile apart. The amplitude of the seismic waves that each created was recorded in Alaska. Significantly, those of 2003 arrived just fractionally more quickly than those of 1993 implying that the very center of the Earth spins at a faster rate than Earth's surface. This may be highly significant. Disturbance at Earth's very core must play a key role in the shifting of tectonic plates which, in turn, leads to Earth movement recognized in tsunamis, volcanic eruption, and earthquake. As earth is literally "moved" so too are minerals. The effect of magnetism on the changing composition of the earth must affect all life forms. For example, crops that would not grow in an area may start to do so. The indigenous people of a region may need to acclimatize both to changed food and local water supply.

As Earth's core is affected by solar activity—and not always manifesting in earth upheaval and perhaps working at more subtle level—it may be that human behavior too is affected, and that this in turn has influence on activity in global markets.

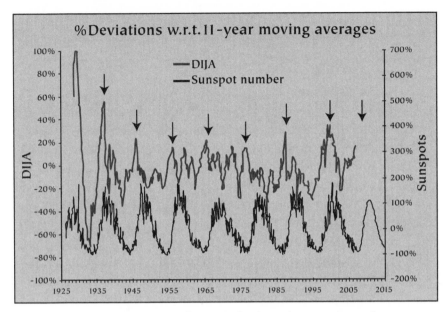

Data source: T. Modis, in *Technological Forecasting and Social Change* (2007) www.wattsupwiththat.com

Astro-economists have looked for correlation between the number of sunspots and stock market indices. The results are compelling. The graph above was prepared during the recent extended minima period and showed an extended peak in 2014.

As the number of sunspots increase so too does the level of the Dow Jones stock index. It is entirely to be expected that as solar activity increases, so too do the hopes of market traders—pushing indices ever higher.

EFFECT ON PEOPLE

As yet, it is not possible to forecast all solar activity. My clients do appreciate being reminded of solar rhythms and of possible consequences in trading however.

I have worked with investors who were born when sunspot activity was extremely low. In tracing their investment history we discovered that they had made their best decisions when the numbers were similarly low and their worst when the numbers were very high. It may be that we each operate at our best when solar conditions match those at our birth. Sunspot tables can be found in Neil Michelson's excellent book, *Planetary Phenomena* or through the NASA website.

Neil Michelson's book also lists major magnetic storms. Allow a short orb for their influence. Another two investors were both born within 24 hours of major storms—which seems to hint at their propensity to suddenly "seize on the moment" and to take risks that others might consider foolhardy. Both are exceptionally good investors.

This is by no means a piece of solid research but rather an interesting observation.

Solar activity clearly affects Earth as a whole. Yet it can also be shown that solar activity affects particular locations on Earth.

Astrogeography

In recent years, a technique known as astro-geography has gained popularity among astrologers. What they have noted is that individuals behave differently depending on where they are living. By moving from the place of birth to a new latitude or longitude, the role of the various planets, Sun and Moon is amplified or reduced. This should be of great interest to both investors and traders as it may be that they find they work better with some markets more than others.

This fits well with the work of Dr. Ellsworth Huntingdon who opined that the optimum temperature for human performance was 38F for mental activity and 68–70F for physical activity. It is quite possible that not only might the investor or trader benefit from being in a different "place" on earth but that performance is affected by the weather systems of the region.

Recent research has shown that the latitude of birth and the amount of solar radiation you were exposed to while still in the womb has distinct bearing on your life journey.

As we know, the Sun emits ultraviolet rays which have effect on the genetic changes in developing babies and subsequently on their life span. It can be shown that those born in the month of

December and in the Northern hemisphere have a greater chance of celebrating their 100th birthday than those born in the month of June. This research, carried out by the Rostock University in Germany was supported by that of another study at the University of Chicago which showed that those born in December lived an average of three years longer than those born six months earlier.

The University of Maine conducted a survey on well-being, and found that those born between latitudes 53N and 54N had significantly higher possibility of being creative. Other studies show how different latitudes affect the probability of experiencing certain diseases.

It would appear that the key influence is the amount of solar radiation experienced pre-birth. Generally, latitudes close to the Equator and the Equator itself experience maximum radiation which, in the Northern hemisphere, peaks in June and December.

A possibility is that high radiation levels stress the immune systems of embryos and foetuses causing small but vital mutations in DNA. It may be that those born in December (and so conceived around March) avoid the most harmful radiation at the very start of their incubation.

The Maine study—while dismissing astrology—showed that the actual time of year of birth (and therefore the Sun's position) together with actual latitude of birth, determined predisposition to certain diseases and propensity to certain characteristics.

The amount of solar radiation varies with the sunspot cycle of course. The Maine study looked at births over seven sunspot cycles determining that overall disease rates were 28% higher in those born during peak radiation periods.

Yet another study—this time by researchers at St Andrew's University—showed that some of the greatest creative mathematicians were conceived around the Summer Solstice. They showed also that over the past 400 years, 54% of acknowledged (famous) mathematicians were born at latitude 53N.

In terms of personality, a study by the University of Umea in Sweden found that those born between February and April (covering the signs Aquarius, Pisces and Aries) were more likely to be novelty seekers than those born between October and

December (Libra, Scorpio and Sagittarius). We might wonder if those born with the Sun in Aquarius, Pisces or Aries have particular aptitude for risk management and, perhaps, trading. Further study awaits.

This list of websites is not comprehensive but offers a useful starting point:

www.spaceweather.com

www.solarcycle24.com

http://www.cxoadvisory.com/calendar-effects/sunspot-cycle-and-stock-returns/

Reference:

http://www.cyclesresearchinstitute.org/cycles-history/chizhevsky1.pdf

IN CONCLUSION

1. The condition of the Sun—both at birth and its current condition—should be considered by all traders and investors. It might also suit some of these people to move to areas where they feel they will experience optimum performance.
2. Following the Sun's recent retrograde period, many people are on the move, driven from their homes by both climate change and conflict. This situation is unlikely to stabilize until there is distinct change in solar behavior. The number of sunspots in Cycle 24 has been low. Cycles 25 and 26 could be even lower. This in turn could lead to mass migration with many people returning to lands left just a decade before.
3. Taking into account both solar activity as shown by Cycle 24, and understanding of Professor Wheeler's study, it seems reasonable to forecast that we are in a period of transition and that the changing weather patterns of the coming years will

have huge importance and impact on our lives whether we are traders or not.

4. While it may not be possible to protect ourselves from catastrophe in the form of power outage caused by solar storm, we should all ensue we have a solid network of friends and neighbours on whom we can rely in the event of disaster.

5. Short-term traders could add the solar flux index to their arsenal of trading tools. Investors might also take into account that businesses incorporated at latitudes 53–54N may have local employees with particular gifts in mathematics, and the technology systems built on this talent.

There are, no doubt, a myriad of ways in which understanding of solar activity could be of use to both traders and investors. Key though is acknowledging the importance of solar activity.

CHAPTER TWO

THE GLOBAL FINANCIAL CRISIS FROM 2007

There aren't many generations who can say that they lived through a global financial crisis. The end of the first decade of the 21st century brought conditions unfamiliar to many. This, of course, was part of the problem. Economists could look back to the early 1930s and the Great Depression, while politicians vowed that there would be no repeat of those times. Yet many people had little to no understanding of the dynamics that led to those earlier disasters. The majority—bankers and traders included— were blissfully unaware that situations were developing at such a rate that a meltdown of both global trade and financial systems would be hard to avert.

Even today it is said that few saw this coming. Actually, those looking to the heavens and studying the cycles of the planets had intimated for many years that this period could coincide with difficulties in trading systems that might well bring international trading systems to the brink. Of these forecasters, those with understanding of market operating methods wondered if earlier decisions—especially those moves taken between 1981 and 1990 —would come back to haunt those who had devised them.

In 1981, Pluto arrived in the sign of Scorpio—the sign with which it is said to have greatest affinity. Those monitoring the movement of the planets through the heavens have arrived at the conclusion that when planets pass through certain areas (signs or specific degree areas), there is more noticeable effect than at other times.

Within months of Pluto's arrival in Scorpio, Jupiter and Saturn formed a conjunction in Libra: the first time they had aligned in an Air sign of the zodiac for some hundreds of years (January 1405). The effect on global markets was obvious. Prices rose (wealth building) while volatility (Airy ideas) increased.

Financial astrologers were of the opinion that when Pluto arrived in Capricorn (2008), the global financial system would—

at the very least—be subject to major upheaval. "Castles in the Air" would be sent tumbling if the structures underpinning them were unsafe. At the very least it was likely that a shake-up in the way in which taxes are collected was probable: this made necessary by increased global trade and the difficulties created for governments in securing tax revenue.

Pluto is the planet associated with profound upheaval and transition, and the sign of Capricorn is linked to large structures, governments, major institutions, and, in particular, the wealth of nations. In a sense then, what took place in 2007–11 is astrologically understandable.

At the time of writing, Pluto is only half way through the sign of Capricorn. Global financial markets have most likely not even reached the "interval" in this particular show, which ends when Pluto moves from Capricorn and on into Aquarius (2024). This "interval" is likely to come when Pluto reaches the very delicate area of 17–19 Capricorn in 2017–18. As might be expected at any theatre show, what happens just before the interval is the cliff-hanger that starts the second half.

To assess what may yet take place in the coming decade requires that we review some of the key dates since Pluto arrived in Capricorn.

As we shall see in our study of difficult periods for markets in the 20th century, it is clear that it is not just the sign in which planets travel that has relevance. Also of importance are the unfolding of the cycles of each planetary pair and other planetary formations—such as the Grand Cross (where four planets are at apparent right-angles to one another), the Grand Trine (where three are apparently equidistant), and other planetary shapes.

2000–2010

As the first decade of the 21st century drew to a close, two cycles in particular reached critical phase: Saturn and Uranus opposed one another, while Uranus and Pluto arrived at their first quarter. The former aspect occurs roughly every 45 years, while the latter is experienced every two centuries. At this first quarter or apparent right-angle, both Uranus and Pluto would occupy Cardinal signs of the zodiac. As viewed from Earth, Saturn and Uranus would form no fewer than five oppositions with the last also in Cardinal signs. Together all this promised a period of high drama affecting the arenas of politics, economics and societies generally.

Those studying these cycles from 2000, noted that these major aspects or angles would follow Pluto's transit of the Galactic Center, and that both Saturn and Uranus would reach right angles to this degree—adding to the high probability of a global crisis of some kind.

THE GALACTIC CENTER

It is not known what, exactly, is at the center of our galaxy, the Milky Way. There may well be a Black Hole. Certainly it seems that this is a dense area of high energy. As planets align with this degree (roughly 27 Sagittarius), their respective energies seem to increase. Thus it could be said that Pluto becomes "more Pluto" at this crossing and, if Pluto is about upheaval, then this suggests upheaval at nuclear or devastating scale.

Of course it could—and should—be argued that rot in the global financial system set in well before 2007, when lax regulation allowed conditions to develop to the point where collapse became inevitable. It might even be that had regulations been put in place as Pluto passed the Galactic Center, then there would have been a reduction in the financial pain experienced by many.

What we all know now is that the crisis came about as a direct result of the sub-prime mortgage market in the US where loans were given to people who had neither significant credit history nor the prospect of being able to repay. At best this would be described as a nebulous market where documentation was poor and adequate credit checks left unaudited.

Between 1984 and 1998 Neptune made its passage through Capricorn. Its 14-year-long passage through this sign will not recur until 2148 and its last passage through that sign was between 1820 and 1834. The end of this latter period witnessed a banking collapse that echoes those of recent times.

In the early years of the 19th century, private banks had a license to print money that was not backed by physical reserves. Unsustainable lending, rampant inflation, and governments which had to bail out these private banks eventually led to crisis (1837).

A decade before Neptune concluded its passage through Capricorn, Uranus arrived in this same sign. Uranus is the planet associated with the drive to "do things differently" so it is perhaps unsurprising that the usual formulas for credit management were abandoned as that planet moved through this sign.

What might best be described as "unusual and obfuscated" financial systems (derivatives, credit default swaps etc.) gained momentum. Indeed, these became ever more complex from 2003 when Uranus and Neptune moved into what is termed "mutual reception," i.e. when each planet is in a sign favored by the other.

Those who had even vague understanding of these markets were no doubt alarmed. Those with knowledge of the cycles of the planets were more so: viewing Pluto's approach to both the Galactic Center and then to the sign of Capricorn as being akin to approaching steel buffers. There was very real concern that huge problems would have to be faced and that the unravelling of complex financial practices might take years—or at least until the opposition of Saturn and Uranus (also due at the end of this first decade)—was in the past. The "crisis" may indeed last far longer—possibly until after the next Jupiter-Saturn conjunction in 2020.

THE CRACKS BEGIN TO SHOW and SIX EXAMPLES OF FINANCIAL STRESS

Example 1

On August 9, 2007, (see chart page 31), the bank BNP Paribas announced that it was ceasing activity in three hedge funds specializing in US mortgage debt. Notably, it was around this date that Pluto aligned with the Galactic Center. Astro-economists had long held the view that this placement would coincide with deep (Plutonic) shocks in global trading. What the investor would have wanted to know is whether or not the actual date could be forecast. Certainly, aware that Pluto was both passing the Galactic Center and en route to Capricorn, the astrologer might well have been looking for signs of potential malfunction. Pluto though is a slow moving planet that takes many months to pass over any particular degree. Astro-economists waiting for signs of pending collapse, were looking for a "trigger": the arrival of another planet at significant position which might prompt the drama to unfold.

On August 9, 2007, Saturn formed a trine (120 degree aspect) to Pluto. This might normally be considered a positive aspect. However, that same day, Uranus, our "planet of the unexpected" was at 17 Pisces. This position is exactly opposite one of the most critical degrees areas in the chart for the New York Stock Exchange. As we shall see in subsequent chapters, 17 degrees of Virgo, and its opposite sign, Pisces, are fragile areas for Wall Street indices in particular. Yet Uranus too is a relatively slow moving planet and although the financial astrologer might have looked at this first week of August as being potentially difficult, it would not have been the only period under scrutiny as Uranus would be close to this degree for some months.

To determine exactly when cracks in the system might show, the financial astrologer looked deeper: focusing on the movements of faster-moving planets.

Interestingly, in early August, Jupiter lay exactly half way between the lunar south and north Nodes: most likely signalling a market top. It is not at all abnormal for Jupiter's position, at tight angle with the Moon's nodal axis to coincide with increased market activity and market tops. In the days following squares, oppositions, or conjunctions of Jupiter and the Node—and whatever the signs involved—indices tend to fall.

Full focus though would be given to the Sun's opposition to Chiron on the Monday of that August week. It might even be that the decision to withdraw from these funds was taken then.

Those working for BNP Paribas would have been aware of the bank's exposure to many trillions of dollars' worth of questionable derivative value and would surely have been working for some weeks to avert what they would have known would be a decision with enormous ramification. As we now know, their decision was

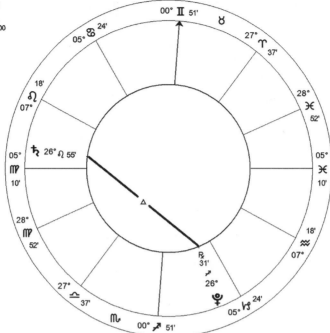

BNP PARIBAS
Natal Chart
Aug 9 2007, Thu
9:00 am CEDT −2:00
MADRID, SPAIN
40°N24' 003°W41'
Geocentric
Tropical
Placidus
True Node

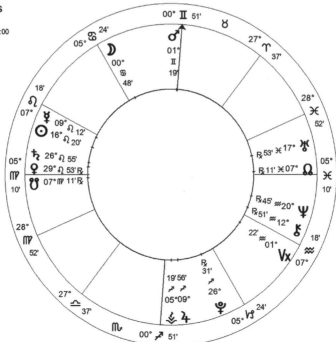

BNP PARIBAS
Natal Chart
Aug 9 2007, Thu
9:00 am CEDT −2:00
MADRID, SPAIN
40°N24' 003°W41'
Geocentric
Tropical
Placidus
True Node

perhaps just the first in a series that caused trust between banks to break down. Even today, what passed for "normal service" has not yet resumed.

Far more importantly, however, are a series of midpoints which, cumulatively, pointed directly to this date. As before, the focus is on the links between the so-called "outer" planets. The midpoint system works as follows: a planet (A) placed either at the half-way point of the shorter or longer arc between two planets (B & C) is considered to be at "the midpoint" of the two planets. The works of Alfred Witte, Charles Harvey, Mike Harding, and Michael Munkasey shows that even if Planet A is in any multiple of 45 degrees from the half-way point of either the shorter or longer arc it is considered to be on that midpoint.

The midpoint alignments or "pictures," as they are known, for any date are complex. In this instance however, one stands out: Uranus was at the midpoint of Jupiter and Pluto. The cycle of this pair is often termed the "wealth cycle." With Uranus at this exact midpoint, the image conjured up would be of a deep shock affecting the system. Meanwhile, Saturn was at the midpoint of Jupiter and Chiron: a picture that suggested the cosmic headmaster (Saturn) demanding that any over-optimistic tendencies (Jupiter) be addressed (Chiron).

Financial astrologers then were well aware that this period was likely to be eventful. They would be further alarmed by the parallel aspect between Mercury and Mars operative that day.

Once a period is under review, final confirmation of probable activity usually comes from aspects made by the Sun and Moon. Note that the Sun moves at a rate of approximately one degree per day. It may be thought of as the ward of the clock. On August 9, 2007, the Sun moved to the direct midpoint of Neptune and Chiron, demanding that any losses be faced—even if they could not, at that stage, be quantified.

If the astro-coding within the charts for early August 2007 seemed a little obscure, the same cannot be said for the next key date associated with the global financial crisis: September 15, 2008. Between August 2007 and September 2008, Saturn and Uranus moved to their opposition phase. This cycle pits the past against the future and, at approximately 45-year intervals, demands that systems be reviewed. In 2007–08, the two planets opposed one another across the Virgo-Pisces axis—just as they had been in March 1966 when major indices across the world suffered major losses. The chart below is that of the March Full Moon in 1966. The Full Moon occurred in the early hours of that morning, and the Moon had moved by a few degrees by the time European markets opened. The Moon was moving into square aspect with Jupiter that morning forming a T-square with the Sun, Saturn, and Chiron opposing Uranus, Pluto, and the Moon—and with Jupiter half-way between these major oppositions.

Indeed, though the exact planetary picture for 1966 was not replicated in 2008, there was sufficient similarity with that Full Moon—when markets faltered before falling substantially—for astro-economicsts to be concerned about a likely repeat of loss. One of the striking features of the 1966 event is that Saturn and Uranus held degree areas known to be highly significant for the New York Stock Exchange in particular. With Saturn (pessimism)

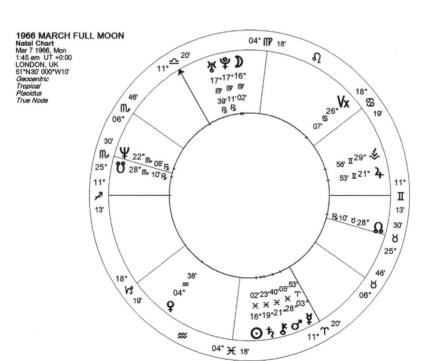

1966 MARCH FULL MOON
Natal Chart
Mar 7 1966, Mon
1:45 am UT +0:00
LONDON, UK
51°N30' 000°W10'
Geocentric
Tropical
Placidus
True Node

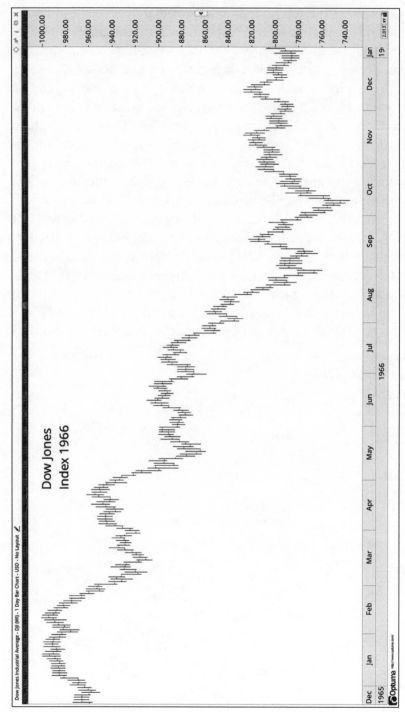

Dow Jones Index 1966

on one of these degrees and Uranus (shocks) opposing this, it was perhaps not so surprising that early March 1966 proved so very eventful as can be seen in this graph of Dow Jones Index trading in the first half of that year.

Example 2

Again mirroring March 1966, on September 15, 2008, the Full Moon was within just a few degrees of the planet Uranus: suggesting a day of high volatility. If history was to repeat, this would surely prove a day of high volatility—which indeed proved to be the case.

In fact, the situation was far worse than that of 1966. There were many astro-reasons for this: most notably Pluto's presence in Capricorn which shifted attention to the wealth and banking system of nations.

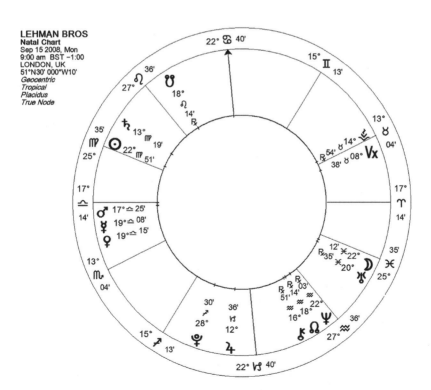

The significance of Mercury and Venus aligning at 19 degrees of one of the Cardinal signs was not lost on financial astrologers. Their historical analysis of earlier stock market crashes alerted them to the high probability of severe—and negative—market reaction that day. They would also have been highly concerned about the Chiron-Node exact conjunction (one of the major configurations that took place in the autumn of 1929).

This Full Moon, within orb of conjunction with the Uranus, was to mark the start of an extremely messy and untidy autumn. No one knew for sure that deals struck in the fortnight post this Full Moon would stick. Would governments bail-out the banks and if so, which banks would cease to operate. This is perhaps understandable given that Mercury turned retrograde on September 24th, crossing then re-crossing 19 Libra. In keeping with this transit, there was outright confusion as politicians and bankers sought ways to avert a total global economic collapse. In the end, there was to be no bail-out for Lehman Brothers as there had been for both Bear Stearns in the US and Northern Rock in the UK.

From the astro-perspective, we can say that Uranus "won" and that Saturn "lost." With Saturn there is emphasis on preserving the status quo, whereas with Uranus, the status quo has no currency and even the unknown is embraced. What was clear to all was that this was no repeat of 1929 and that the stakes in 2008 were higher than they had ever been: a total global economic collapse could still occur.

True, banks were rescued but even this was not enough to stop the global economy moving into unchartered and potentially dangerous waters. A new phrase entered into economic vocabulary as conditions were eased through "quantitative easing": the creation of electronic money. Though several planetary pictures may be used to describe this concept, it is fitting that the idea was born as Uranus (deviant and original) moved through Pisces (masterfully creative).

The geocentric opposition of Saturn and Uranus was mathematically exact on five occasions between November 2008 and July 2010. The last of these took place across the Aries-

Libra axis and the earlier ones across Virgo-Pisces. It is perhaps accurate to say that by the time the last of these was reached in July 2010, the global financial world had entered entirely new territory. It may also prove to be the case that the decisions taken between November 2008 and June 2010 have long-lasting and, perhaps, chaotic effect.

Virgo and Pisces are two of the Mutable signs of the zodiac. On December 24, 2014, Saturn made its next entry into a mutable sign (Sagittarius) and in 2016 will have moved a full 90 degrees from the 2008–10 positions. This too could prove a critical period when once again the accent is on accountability.

Example 3

Soon after the March 2009 Equinox, the G20 leaders gathered in London and, on April 2nd, announced measures amounting to commitment to the creation of $5 trillion for fiscal expansion coupled with a determination to reform the banking system.

Of the many features of this chart: the close conjunction of Chiron (problem-solving) to Neptune (everything!) is perhaps not so surprising. Reform of the banking industry is shown in the right-angle (square) between Venus and Pluto. The cycle of these two planets has become exceedingly important since 2009. During the course of the year, they form a conjunction, two squares and an opposition. Significant "banking stories" have hit the headlines within a day or so of the formation of each of these angles.

It is time to introduce a new "character" to the chart. The asteroid Vesta (whose glyph appears as a small flame), has held prominent positions at times of financial eventfulness and is usually prominently placed in the charts of traders and financiers.

During the April 2009 short conference, Vesta was in square angle to both Chiron and Neptune. Two weeks earlier, Vesta was at right-angles to Jupiter. Presumably the world leaders and their finance ministers who later attended the event, faced with the realization of just how great the problems were, determined that

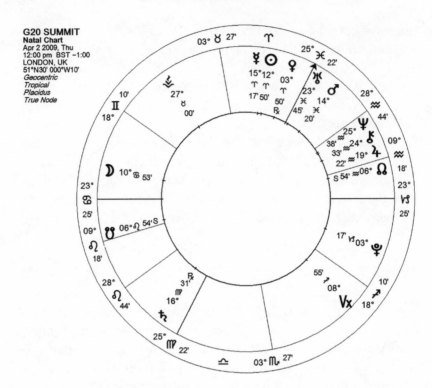

they really must attend. This was quite a remarkable event in that the conference was put together very much at the last minute.

The conference was held as the Sun moved through Aries and, as we have noted, with Chiron and Neptune in close conjunction. The need to somehow magically (Neptune) make corrections (Chiron) and to do so in a bold (Sun in Aries) way was surely very strong.

Yet inevitably, individuals states and nations focused on their particular needs so that, far from resolving issues, difficulties were set to escalate. Chiron and Neptune in Aquarius played a planetary theme of "working for the common good" but, as the two separated, this hope dissolved as the complex realities of the situation became known. Soon emphasis would turn from the strength or otherwise of particular banks to the actual creditworthiness of nations.

Example 4

The IMF and European Union announced on May 9, 2010 that they would provide financial assistance to Greece.

In May 2010, Uranus had reached the very last degree of Pisces. Faster-moving Jupiter (the rescuer) was within weeks of forming a conjunction with this planet while Saturn, retrograde, was within minutes of a degree opposition to Uranus. Of course there was an urgency (Uranus in the last degree of a sign) to the situation and certainly those involved were acutely aware that without a bail-out the system would fail—with huge and detrimental effect on many.

Note that Saturn was at exact 150 degree angle from Neptune (the quincunx). This is an important aspect or angle that usually brings eventfulness. You can think of this as two planes on different flight paths having to take quick action to avoid collision. It was probably felt that bitter medicine would need to be taken by the populace for the entire system to survive.

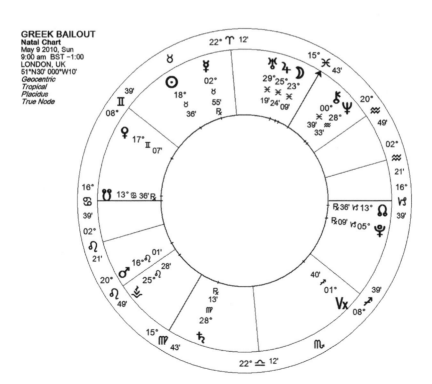

GREEK BAILOUT
Natal Chart
May 9 2010, Sun
9:00 am BST −1:00
LONDON, UK
51°N30' 000°W10'
Geocentric
Tropical
Placidus
True Node

Ahead of both Saturn and Uranus changing signs (as they would do in July 2010), Chiron had made its Pisces ingress. The passage of a planet from one sign to another (an ingress) brings a change of pace and emphasis in new areas. It was certainly fitting that with Chiron's entry into Pisces that weakness would be exposed.

Why Greece? All countries have "birth charts"—with most having several. Each of these charts or horoscope marks a new stage in the political, social and economic lives of the peoples of an area. In the most recent chart for Greece, there is a Moon Pluto conjunction at 4 degrees of Libra. As Pluto, at 5 Libra, squared these degrees in 2009 and the early part of 2010, Greece's resource cupboard was found to be bare. In keeping with a theme often apparent when Pluto is at work, there was grave concern as to how the taxation system did or did not work.

The IMF gave Greece a deadline of June 30, 2015 to make a repayment. As can be seen in the chart below, the Nodal axis—

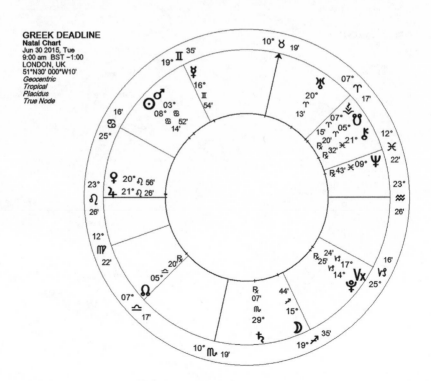

GREEK DEADLINE
Natal Chart
Jun 30 2015, Tue
9:00 am BST −1:00
LONDON, UK
51°N30' 000°W10'
Geocentric
Tropical
Placidus
True Node

exact on the degrees of the Moon's Node-Pluto conjunction—was at 5 Libra-Aries, with Mars in Cancer at a right angle to this axis.

If these degrees remain sensitive then we should expect major developments in this on-going financial tale as planets pass 5–6 degrees of Aries or Libra or square this axis at 5–6 Capricorn. Of the relatively slow-moving planets, Saturn crosses 5–6 Capricorn in 2019. If matters are not resolved by then (as seems unlikely), then this period too could find the Greek government faced with very difficult choices.

Example 5

The next date to be given consideration was August 5th 2011 when Standard and Poor's rating agency reduced the US credit rating.

Much comment was made of the fact that the announcement of the credit down-grading was made *after* the markets had closed: presumably to avoid over-reaction to the news. The

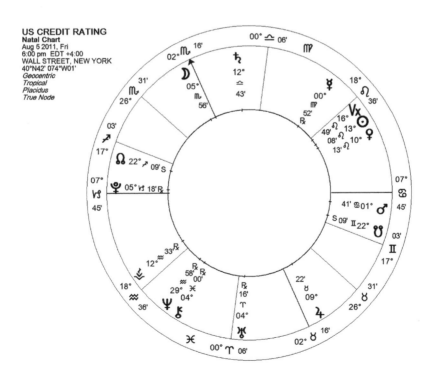

US CREDIT RATING
Natal Chart
Aug 5 2011, Fri
6:00 pm EDT +4:00
WALL STREET, NEW YORK
40°N42' 074°W01'
Geocentric
Tropical
Placidus
True Node

announcement was made late on a Friday giving traders the weekend to think about the implications. It may be said that the date was chosen with care—with full awareness of the likely impact this would have.

It is striking that during the course of the following week— the exact time-frame when reaction was most likely to be seen— Mars, (recently moved into Cancer), moved to oppose Pluto with Uranus at the midpoint of the two. Highly significant is that Mars at this point in its declination cycle was "out of bounds"—a feature of its journey around the Sun that is not an annual event. In this instance, Mars acted as a trigger to the long-term aspect between the two slower-moving planets. Even without this announcement financial astrologers were on alert for unusual activity: with the announcement they were assured that market movements would be substantial.

Of course they noted that the Sun had just left the opposition to Vesta: which, with the benefit of hindsight, speaks of the pre-planning that would have taken place before the announcement. Another interesting aspect is that of Venus at right-angle to Jupiter just ahead of that news. This potent combination of planetary pictures coincided with major aspects affecting the horoscope of the United States—underscoring the probability of American markets experiencing volatility that week.

Many argued that this down-grading of US credit should not have been taken at all Some felt that the figures used were suspect. It comes as little surprise then that Mercury, at the very edge of Virgo and in opposition to Neptune was retrograde. The signals were very confusing indeed.

Example 6

What was neither nebulous nor confusing was the decisive action taken in March 2013 when Cyprus was declared bankrupt and when many citizens lost their savings: their funds were taken to make part pay-off of loans taken out by the country's banks. Whereas the situation in Greece was exceedingly serious yet a combination of austerity and bail-out resulted in that coun-

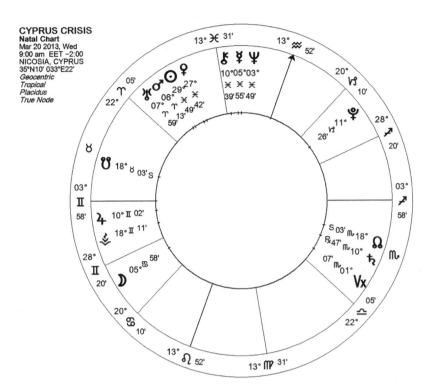

CYPRUS CRISIS
Natal Chart
Mar 20 2013, Wed
9:00 am EET −2:00
NICOSIA, CYPRUS
35°N10' 033°E22'
Geocentric
Tropical
Placidus
True Node

try staying financially afloat for a few years, the same options were not given to Cyprus where banks were closed for many days and where some citizens lost vast sums of legitimately accrued savings.

The chart for the Cyprus crisis offers understanding as to why moves made were so decisive and why a period of grace was not offered:

As earlier studies have shown, major aspects involving Chiron seem to coincide with periods of marked correction. On March 20, 2013—and as the Sun arrived at the Equinox (one of the four most important dates of the year), Jupiter and Chiron were at an exact right-angle. As importantly, Jupiter was at the apex of a configuration known as a "Finger of God" or "Fated angle" where two other planets were each equidistant from it. The two base planets of this special isosceles triangle were Saturn and Pluto: both slow moving planets. It is unusual to find Jupiter,

Saturn and Pluto in this formation. Those looking to the heavens and seeing the planets move into this formation thought that the day of exactitude of the aspect might be a day of international (Jupiter) administrative (Saturn) determined action (Pluto) the consequences of which would reverberate for many decades.

It is worth noting too that on the day itself, Mars and Uranus were conjunct: an event that occurs every two years but which, coinciding with the Equinox, was likely to result in singular activity. Certainly the planetary conditions of this period were extraordinary.

By examining these five key dates—and yes, there are others that could be considered—it is possible to build up a profile of the planetary signatures that might determine significant market movements in the future. The backdrop to all this is, of course, Pluto's transit of the sign of Capricorn. It was always reasonable to expect that greatest change and dynamic events would occur as Uranus made its right angle to this planet in the years 2011–15. What is clear is that as any of the faster moving planets oppose or square either of these planets, there is increased volatility.

Mars takes a little over two years to travel through all twelve signs while Uranus takes approximately 84 years to orbit the Sun. The Mars-Uranus opposition then takes place more or less every second year. Since 2000, Mars opposed Uranus (geocentrically) in the Augusts of 2000, 2002, 2004, 2006, and 2008, and then in July of both 2010 and 2012 before the triple series in 2013/2014.

When Mars opposes Uranus, a market top is likely. This rarely happens on the day when the aspect is exact and is usually triggered by another event. Thanks to retrograde periods, the aspect can occur more than once in the space of a few months. In 2014 the aspect occurred three times and only on the last was a top reached.

CHAPTER THREE

OUTER PLANET ALIGNMENTS AND STOCK MARKET CRASHES

In this chapter we will look at the ten "worst" stock market crashes since 1900 and observe the different planetary signatures involved in each. The aim in this chapter is to observe the conditions both at the start and finish of each period of loss. As we study these events, we will also consider when there might be a "re-enactment" allowing us to forecast future periods of instability.

While individual planetary cycles repeat regularly (Sun-Moon every month, Mars-Uranus about every two years, Jupiter-Saturn every 20 years, for example), their placement in the zodiac, and the phases of other cycles, taken together, only repeat about every 26,000 years. Even then, the repetition is not exact. Consequently each stock market "crash" has its own exact planetary signature. Yet we find that when similar themes, similar planetary configurations, are at work, traders (and then markets) react in the same way.

This chapter then offers an exercise in astro-detection where we will discover areas of the zodiac that are high profile when markets across the world lose value and the phases of specific planetary cycles form the backdrop for such events.

Before moving on we should recall that Pluto was not discovered until 1930 and it was 1977 when Chiron, the planetoid orbiting between Saturn and Uranus was added to our charts. Only since 1977 has the link between the Chiron-Pluto cycle and major market moves been discerned. This goes some way to explain why the track record of financial astrologers in the last fifty years has been superior to that of their forebears. The limitations unconsciously experienced by early astrologers demanded that they pay more attention to the shorter cycles of the Sun, Mercury, Venus and Mars in particular. As we shall see, the discovery of Chiron and Pluto and calculation of their respective orbits and positions has led to increased understanding of the "bigger

45

picture" and why some periods of negative activity last longer than others.

1900–1905

Analysis of sunspot activity from 1900–05 shows numbers to have been extremely low. Low solar activity often coincides with high crop prices as demand exceeds supply. With the benefit of hindsight and understanding of solar cycles it was to be expected that the opening years of the 20th century would be economically difficult: as was the case.

Over 46% of the value of stocks was lost in the near 30-month period between June 1901 and November 1903 when a severe drought in the US promoted alarm over rising food prices. Many regard this as being the first crash experienced by the New York Stock Exchange (NYSE). (Note that in the opening chapter, it was suggested that another severe drought will be experienced between 2019 and 2021 at the next solar minima.)

The opening years of the 20th century encompassed an opposition of Uranus and Pluto: a planetary picture indicating profound (Pluto) and sudden upheaval (Uranus). It is acknowledged by astrologers that when these two planets are either conjunct, at apparent right angles, in opposition, or when they share degrees of declination, then disruption—and even chaos—is likely. At best, these angles coincide with exercises in redeployment of resources.

Though, as explained, Pluto was not discovered until 1930, its position at any time prior to that year can be calculated. Major aspects i.e. conjunctions, squares (90 degrees), and oppositions (180 degrees) of Uranus and Pluto occurring since the 18th century include, 1756, 1792–03, 1820–21, 1850, 1876, 1901–02, 1932, 1965, and between 2010 and 2015.

The opposition between Uranus and Pluto through 1901–03 had last occurred in 1793—coinciding with revolution in France. It is never enough to note only the aspects (angles) between any two planets but it is also important to note exactly where in the zodiac aspects took place. In 1793 Uranus was in the sign of Leo, and Pluto was moving through the opposite sign of Aquarius. The actual signs involved indicate the likely theatres in which action will be played out. (Leo has connection with royalty and Aquarius with the "common man"—fitting symbolism for the revolution in France of that period.)

The next opposition will occur between 2046 and 2048 and, as with these other periods, will no doubt coincide with sharp upheaval and correction in market indices. The signs involved then will be Virgo and Pisces suggesting that the sector most likely to experience great loss will be that of bio-technics, pharmaceuticals and, most probably, energy.

In 1901, the two planets opposed one another from Gemini to Sagittarius, the two signs associated with communication, connections, and travel. It should come as little surprise that it was investments in the growing railroad system in the USA that bore the brunt of losses.

The first of five (geocentric) oppositions of Uranus to Pluto took place in late January 1901 and the last in November 1902. Equities began to lose value with the first of these geocentric oppositions and continued to fall for a further twelve months *after* the last of these oppositions took place.

We should first ask why recovery did not happen sooner. If we accept that the Uranus-Pluto opposition is destabilising, why was there no immediate improvement when the two planets moved away from this angle?

To understand this we must look to another cycle that demands frequent attention when analysing periods of poor economic activity: the cycle of planetoid Chiron and the Lunar Node.

Chiron may be the remnant of a trapped comet. It has been described as the "wounded healer" and holds prominent position in the charts of those for whom the medical profession has particular significance. Yet it seems important too in the charts of auditors and accountants. It appears to act as some sort of "adjuster." As we shall see, Chiron's position on, opposite, or at right angles to the Lunar Nodes marks a likely correction in the marketplace.

As Uranus (the faster moving planet) drew away from the opposition with Pluto, Chiron and the Node were moving into a

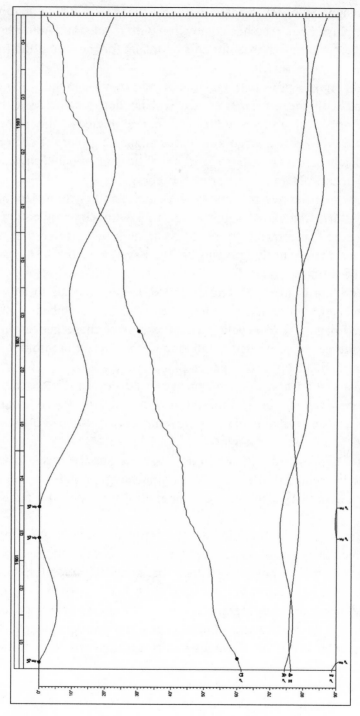

1901–1903 with Quarters marked and showing Uranus–Pluto aspects and Chiron–Node crossing square relationship with one another: the angle becoming exact on February 10, 1903—at 19 degrees of Cancer.

To illustrate this, consider the graph opposite (known as a graphic ephemeris). In this instance, a 90-degree version of the ephemeris is used. Where planetary lines cross we know the planets concerned must be either conjunct, in opposition (twice 90 degrees or 180 degrees), or in square (at 90 degrees) from one another. Here we can see Uranus and Pluto (the lines close to the bottom of the graph) criss-crossing one another. Each crossing marks an opposition between the two planets.

The line moving from the left hand side of the graph to the top right, is the Lunar Node which moves backwards through the zodiac. It crosses Chiron's line, marking the square between them, in February 1903.

As viewed from Earth, planets—and Chiron—at times give the appearance of moving backwards. Chiron was retrograde for much of 1903. Significantly, it was after Chiron moved on from 19 Cancer in late November 1903 that stock values increased even though the Chiron-Node right-angle or square aspect concluded at the start of the year.

Study of those crashes since 1900 where over 40% of the value of stocks was lost shows that the axis 19 Cancer-Capricorn (two signs which oppose one another) to be a highly sensitive axis of the zodiac as regards financial matters. Astrologers reading this will be aware that Pluto is presently moving slowly through the latter sign: a fact which says something about the probability of severe market turbulence between 2016 and 2019 when Pluto passes 19 Capricorn.

The opposition of Uranus to Pluto was not the only major cycle at work in 1901–03. During that period, Chiron formed a conjunction with Jupiter and an opposition to Neptune. Let us take a moment to consider the implications of this. Though Jupiter and Neptune oppose one another roughly every 12 years, the opposition of Chiron to Neptune occurs just every 50 or so years. For these two cycles to coincide is rare indeed.

Chiron's opposition to Neptune took place on five occasions between 1900 and 1901. It could be argued that the first of these, in 1900, marked cracks in index values that later became fissures.

(The two did not oppose one another again until 1989/1990. The next opposition of these two bodies occurs in 2048/49.)

History records the period of loss as beginning on June 17, 1901: a few days ahead of the Summer Solstice. The first opposition between Chiron and Neptune occurred 16 months earlier in January 1900, and the first opposition of Uranus and Pluto a year later.

Today's financial astrologer might have advised getting out of the market as 1901 opened—and yes, some loss would no doubt have been incurred by the investor as a result. However, no doubt as the market started to fall, the investor's attention to the astrology of the period might have stirred once more. The investor would be looking for the chance to buy back in.

The closing date of this period of loss is given as November 9, 1903 and the chart shown below. The planetary "picture" for that date is indeed significant. To start with, the Sun was exactly half-way between the Equinox and Solstice. (Gann noted that

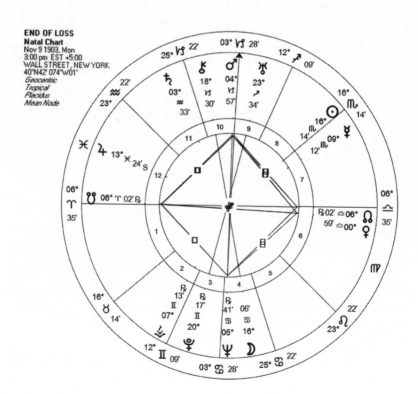

such dates often coincide with a change in market sentiment). That same day, Mars opposed Neptune and the two were at right angles to the Lunar Nodes: forming a Fixed Grand Cross. This would most likely have been identified as a potential bottom or floor. From that date the Dow Jones index rose for some years.

1907

During what is now known as the Panic of 1907, stocks in the US lost over 48% of their value. The crucial dates for this study are January 19, 1906, October 14, 1907, and November 15, 1907.

The dominating astro-theme of 1907 was the opposition of Uranus and Neptune, whose synodic cycle is 179 years. From the geocentric perspective, the aspect occurred 11 times, beginning on March 1, 1906 and concluding in 1910.

Keywords associated with Uranus are sudden, shocking, disruptive, flash, deviant, different, curious, electric, quick, surging, magnetic, technical, brutal, metallic, streaking, urgent, demanding, and eccentric. These words do not fit well with those associated with Neptune which are more to do with illusion, dreams and fantasy. The opposition of the two planets could indeed result in panicked behavior.

Many more people were affected by the panic of 1907 than the financial woes of 1901–03. Astrologically this can be explained by the Uranus opposition to Neptune (1907) rather than Pluto (1901–03). Neptune has widespread effect. If the 1901–03 panic affected institutions and large scale investors, losses were felt as keenly by small-time investors in 1907.

As we saw earlier, planets do not always oppose one another from the same corners of the zodiac. In 1906, Uranus was in Capricorn while Neptune was in Cancer. Capricorn is the sign associated with banking and Cancer with household savings and private investment. Perhaps we should not be surprised that the Panic of 1907 is also known as the Banker's Panic: and yes, there are some parallels here with the global financial crisis of 2008 when it was Pluto's turn to transit through Capricorn.

In 1906, Uranus was at its greatest declination, where it is termed "out of bounds." As is recognized, Uranus has a track record of bringing deviation from the norm. When "out of bounds," that deviation is exaggerated. Panic is an appropriate word for this stock market crash which centered on October 14, 1907 but was clearly growing in the months prior to this.

It is interesting to note that during London market opening hours that day, the Moon was passing 19 Capricorn and aligned with its South Node. As mentioned above, this 18–19 degree of Capricorn is often accented where there is marked market negativity.

As with the bear period of 1901–03, Chiron played a part. Through the autumn of 1907, Jupiter moved to oppose this planetoid. The date given for the end of this loss-making period is, remarkably, the day of their exact opposition—across 13 degrees of, respectively, Leo and Aquarius. On October 14th, the day when greatest losses occurred, Mercury was at right angles to Chiron. This aspect, lasting only a day or so, seems to have been the final trigger that precipitated severe reaction.

Of course, financial astrologers of 1907 would not have known about this aspect and so would be unlikely to have suggested mid-November 1907 as offering "buy" signals. Even so, they might well have chosen a date about a week later when the Sun moved from Scorpio into Sagittarius, aware as they would have been that a change in sign often brings change in market direction.

1916–1917

Aspects between the outer planets, Uranus, Neptune and Pluto, together with those aspects involving the planetoid Chiron, have provided the cosmic background to the periods of economic difficulty in the first decade of the 20th century. Those themes continue through the "crashes" of 1916–17 and 1919–21.

During the thirteen months between November 21, 1916 and December 1917, US stocks lost 40% of their value.

In the earlier examples, Pluto was moving through Gemini. In 1914 Pluto moved into the sign of Cancer. Astrologers recognize that as Pluto moves through this sign there is a strong tendency for people to identify "their territory" and to jealously guard it. Pluto takes nearly a quarter of a millennium to move through all twelve signs. Due to its elongated orbit, it moves through some signs quickly (in just over a decade) and through others signs more slowly (in excess of 20 years). Pluto was in Cancer from 1914 through to 1938. During this period many small investors sought to have a stake in what they believed to be growing industries.

History records stocks as reaching a high on November 21, 1916. On this date, the Lunar Node was at 22 Capricorn. Note that the Node moves backwards through the zodiac at a rate of approximately one degree every three weeks and so was due to reach 19 Capricorn—that very sensitive "financial" zone of the zodiac a few weeks later in January 1917. Had astro-financiers of the time been aware of the financially sensitive nature of this degree area, they would surely have advised extreme caution and, perhaps, suggested moving into cash a few weeks ahead of the alignment. They would also have been aware of the major aspect: the conjunction between Saturn and Neptune forming a backdrop to these years.

Saturn and Neptune form conjunctions approximately every 45 years and their cycle has been termed the "socialist cycle." Defining periods in socialist, labor, and communist development have coincided with major aspects between these two planets. The two conjoined in 1917: the Russian Revolution.

A suitable image for the combination of Saturn and Neptune is a deflating balloon. This combination brings devaluation on a grand cycle. What has been hyped-up will surely be grounded.

Recall that Neptune's entire circuit of the zodiac takes approximately 146 years: thus it spends many years making its passage through each sign. Saturn moves faster (taking around 30 years to make its orbit). The alignment of Saturn and Neptune in Leo is rare. Indeed, prior to 1917, the conjunction last took place in Leo in 1594 and, prior to that, in 1271. Thus the cosmic influences of 1917 were unusual: Saturn's alignment with Neptune in Leo had not been experienced by investors of the period—or by their parents, grandparents or their great-grandparents.

Leo is one of the Fire signs. Saturn is more suited to Earthy Capricorn, and Neptune to Water signs. The presence of both

Saturn and Neptune in this fire sign could be described as sand and water being poured on fire. Within the stock market, hopes were dashed as values fell. Investors in 1915 may have held laudable ideals and great expectations but these surely gave way to crushing disappointment when stocks failed to deliver.

Not only did Saturn and Neptune provide a miserable backdrop to this period, but Chiron was traveling through Pisces during which time it formed a right-angle to the Galactic Center. This angle has, on each occasion in the 20th century, coincided with market negativity.

Perhaps more importantly, Chiron's move into Aries coincided with the Saturn-Neptune conjunction in June 1917: accentuating the probability of cold water being thrown onto investment fires.

The detail:

The astro-historian, while recognizing the likelihood of loss during a particular period, needs to understand the dates which frame it. Precisely what were the planetary conditions which saw a top on November 21, 1916 and which led to stock market growth post-December 19, 1917?

Analysis of great moments in stock market history shows that it is clusters of planetary events that mark specific dates. November 21, 1916 certainly falls into this category. Firstly there was a conjunction and parallel aspect between the Sun and Mercury in late Scorpio. Scorpio is one of the Fixed signs and this alignment could be viewed as a cosmic punctuation mark: a full stop.

On that same date, an "out of bounds" Mars formed a conjunction with Vesta in neighbouring Sagittarius. This is a four year cycle that plays a key role in financial rhythms particularly those involving foreign exchange. With Mars "out of bounds," there was probability of November being a month of high volatility with high probability of stocks exceeding earlier values. The high of that date could probably have been determined in advance even without knowledge of the existence of Pluto or Chiron.

But why then did prices collapse even as the Sun moved on into Sagittarius—another of the Fire signs and one known for being more positive than negative? As values fell it was as though an earthquake hit indices: there were fractures in prices across all sectors.

The driving factor may well have been another angle between Uranus and Pluto: this time that of 135 degrees (a multiple of eighths of a circle and considered to be an action-packed aspect). As this aspect became exact, deep cracks began to show and losses built.

We next turn our attention to December 19, 1917 to see if there were any signals here to identify this as offering a buying opportunity. At first glance the aspects are not obvious: at least not through use of the regular horoscope. If, however, we look at the position of the planets by declination we find a series of important aspects at work.

After this date—and as share values began to increase— Venus moved away from its contra-parallel aspects with Neptune and Pluto. Mercury, which had been out of orb, came back into orb and the Sun began its annual separation from the Galactic Center degree.

It is, of course, quite possible that the financial astrologer would not have isolated this date as being the moment to move back into the market (assuming they'd given the advice to pull out of these investments a year earlier). It is probable though that with the Lunar Node about to cross from Capricorn into Sagittarius, that they might have thought there was high probability that stocks would rise from the end of 1917 and that 1918 would prove a better year.

1919–1921

Between November 3, 1919 and August 24, 1921, stocks lost 46.6% bringing a devastating blow to those who thought that the worst was behind them.

The over-arching aspects of the period 1919–21 were the opposition of Jupiter and Uranus and that of Saturn and Uranus. (Similar aspects were at work during the Dot Com crash at the start of this century as we shall see later).

Recall that with the first "crash" discussed, Saturn and

Uranus were an eighth of a circle apart. They were in multiples of eighths apart from one another in 1909 and in 1915 reaching their opposition phase in 1919. Given that the earlier angles had coincided with negativity in the marketplace, it was always likely that the opposition of the two planets would witness another period of negativity. It might also have been deduced that any negativity would be exaggerated by Jupiter's opposition to Uranus. Though Jupiter moves faster than Saturn, the coinciding effects can be devastating. So it was that the end of one decade and opening of the next witnessed great losses: something we must bear in mind when forecasting the approaching end of decade a century later in 2019.

1929

As we know, the "Roaring 20s" were brought to an abrupt end by the legendary Wall Street Crash in 1929. Nothing was quite as dramatic as that of the fourth quarter of 1929, when the dominating alignment was of Chiron with the North Node—a conjunction which formed on October 23, 1929 at 12 degrees Taurus. This coincided with Mars at the lunar South Node, opposing Chiron, and with Saturn's transit of the Galactic Center. History records October 24th of that year as a day of spectacular loss.

An astro-historian with today's understanding of the solar system, would surely have been concerned as to the possibility of negative trading as Pluto made its passage across 19 Cancer, while Chiron and the Node drew close to conjunction in the autumn of 1929. Having noted outer planet cycle aspects—and Chiron positions in earlier periods of difficulty, he or she might be expected to come to the conclusion that 1929 through 1932 would be a long period of economic discontent and loss.

Yet even financial astrologers of the time—without knowledge or understanding of either Pluto or Chiron's position—were aware of factors at work in 1929 that raised the possibility of a crash.

Firstly, Jupiter formed a conjunction with the Node in May 1929: suggesting a market top. Secondly Mars was out of orb in the first five months of the year neatly concluding this position as

Jupiter and the Node formed their conjunction. An out of bounds Mars is indicative of high energy and high prices. Yet Saturn was moving toward the Galactic Center in late Sagittarius, and it was likely that the closer Saturn moved toward this degree the more weaknesses in the system would be apparent.

Financial astrologers might indeed have singled out the New Moon on September 3rd as being a selling opportunity. This was within hours of Mars' opposition to Uranus. As we shall see, this cycle is often called the "Crash Cycle." Highs are often reached at the opposition before strongly negative moves. Please be aware that this does not happen every time: in every case it is essential to assess all planet cycles and especially those involving the slow-moving planets. Yet this opposition, coinciding with Saturn's approach to the Galactic Center, might have led financial astrologers to advise this as being a time to leave the market place—at least until Saturn had moved beyond this degree.

Those same astrologers might well have identified a buying opportunity mid-November 1929 Indeed, they may have seen this as an excellent purchasing opportunity.

What seems to happen is that as planets move from one sign to another there is a distinct change in human (and therefore market) reaction. Mid-November 1929, Mercury separated from its conjunction with the South Node of the Moon (an expected "low"); Chiron and the North Node too were separating; Venus moved into Scorpio; but, most important of all, Jupiter and Pluto formed a parallel. If Mars-Uranus forms a Crash Cycle, then Jupiter and Pluto offer the possibility of wealth creation.

True, the advisor would still have had some qualms given that Pluto had yet to move on from 19 Cancer. However, it is as likely that study of the movements of the faster moving planets would have led to the conclusion that there might be short term gains to be had: at least while the Node continued its journey through Taurus. That sign change would occur on June 18, 1930—within days of the Summer Solstice and so likely to have great impact.

By the time the Node reached Aries (remember that the Node always moves backwards through the signs), and made hard aspect with some of the outer planets, the position would be very different. Any study of outer planet movement would have resulted in the conclusion that a Great Depression was on the way—particularly as Saturn moved to right angle position with Uranus and opposed Pluto.

Recall, it was the opposition between these two planets that was at work in the earlier crashes. It was always likely that markets would have a similar reaction to the square aspect between the two. Take into account too Saturn's position in Capricorn—and the fact that it would transit over 19 Capricorn, that tender degree area accented in previous crashes. (Note that Saturn crosses this degree area again in 2019.)

Saturn could be described as a "cosmic headmaster." A Saturn transit demands that details are addressed. Cutting corners is not acceptable under Saturn's influence: there is no room for maneuver. There is no buy now, pay later or quantitative easing: Saturn demands that issues are addressed there and then. Austerity and hardship are nearly inevitable. The combination of Saturn with Pluto demands reassessment of resources, hard pruning, and sets the task of living on a shoestring. This is a harsh and unforgiving combination made even more cutting by Uranus' position within this planetary picture. There was little prospect of recovery until Uranus pulled away from the right angle with Pluto, and Saturn moved away from its aspects both with Uranus and Pluto and its opposition with Jupiter.

Economic historians give a date of April 17, 1930 as the start of the Great Depression and set its conclusion as July 8, 1932. Between these dates equities lost 86% of their value; crippling many and leaving some destitute. This period of appalling hardship has left marks on the collective memory and even today, nearly a century later, there is real fear of a return to these times. It is salutary to note that the planetary alignments of 2019–21 has resonance with this earlier period and that we could yet see a period of global financial tensions at the end of this decade.

Assuming that the financial astrologer had indeed suggested climbing back into the market in November: would he or she have noted April 17, 1930—just four short months away—as the moment to sell? Perhaps: Jupiter was retrograde in November. It subsequently stationed and then returned to this degree the following spring. Perhaps the advice to make a few purchases after Jupiter stationed would have been given.

It is perhaps more likely that the astute and well-versed astro-financier would have advised caution and, perhaps, suggested waiting until at least the summer of 1932 by which time the worst of the hard aspects between various outer planets would be concluded.

It is just possible that July 8, 1932 would have been selected as a perfect buying opportunity. Though it is not clear from study of the regular horoscope, even a cursory glance at the declinations of the planets that day shows interesting—and rare—alignments. There was a regular parallel aspect between Mercury and Venus (often a buying opportunity). Decidedly rare though was the triple parallel between the Sun, Mars and Pluto. This could well be viewed as marking a bottom and therefore a potentially ideal date for purchase.

Today, we do have the benefit of hindsight—and knowledge of the position of several major asteroids, including Ceres. It is worth noting that Ceres was in opposition to Pluto for much of this period and that the aspect separated after July 8th.

A word about Ceres: Ceres is the largest of the major asteroids orbiting the Sun between Mars and Jupiter. These may be remnants of another planet. The prominence of Ceres and of another asteroid, Vesta, in the charts of significant financial events cannot be ignored.

Ceres had been known about since the early 19th century when it was discovered by a Sicilian monk. The naming of this orbiting piece of rock is interesting: there is a theme here with the concept of abduction and the lengths a mother will go to to protect her child. There is something of a Persephone and Pluto theme at work. The opposition between Pluto and Ceres could be viewed as a period when the cupboard is bare and when "mother" has nothing left to give. As Ceres, the faster moving of the two objects moves away from this opposition, the nurturing process begins anew and the cupboard is replenished.

Several things are clear from analysis of the five periods of stock market loss so far reviewed. Firstly that a trigger factor is alignment of two or more outer planets or asteroid, with particular regard to the positions of Uranus, Pluto, the Lunar Nodes and Ceres. Secondly, it appears that there is a troublesome degree area around the axis of 19 Cancer-Capricorn.

ECLIPSES

So far there has been no mention of eclipses—either solar or lunar. These certainly yield useful information and assist in the timing of particularly stressful dates: the solar eclipses of 1901–03 were in the signs of Taurus and Scorpio (two signs often associated with financial matters) and in Aries and Libra. The accompanying lunar eclipses took place in those same signs. There was also considerable emphasis on 12 degrees of Taurus and Scorpio (both Fixed signs) which, as with 19 Cancer-Capricorn seem to be a delicate area for finance.

The eclipses of 1906 and 1907 were somewhat different: though again 11 degrees of a Fixed sign (the lunar eclipse of August 1906) was highlighted. The solar eclipse at the start of 1907 was at 22 Capricorn—slightly wide of the 19 degree area but close enough to be regarded as "within orb."

We have now considered five periods where losses greater than 40% were experienced. As we have seen, the actual planetary aspects involved differed. What we can conclude however is that when the outer planets form major aspects—particularly when they are at right angles, opposition, or share declination degrees, traders and investors react in such a way that indices lose value. Just as similar patterns may be shown to coincide with times of war, it seems history continues to repeat whenever these angles form.

1937–1938

The next period of serious loss (49%), occurred between March 1937 and March 1938. It could be concluded that the triggering factor here was Chiron's conjunction with the lunar South Node at the start of April 1937. This was followed by a series of oppositions by Jupiter to Pluto. This latter cycle is relatively short (approximately 12 years). Many economic historians attribute the "crash" of 1937–38 to the decision by the US President to take the dollar off the gold standard.

From a planetary perspective, the key to this being a depressive or negative period is the opposition of Saturn to Neptune and the right angle to both made by Chiron.

The first signal of decline was apparent shortly after the opposition of Mars to Uranus (the "crash" cycle), and as Mars moved from Scorpio to Sagittarius. A financial astrologer would probably have advised sale at the Mars-Uranus opposition or a couple of days before it.

It is fascinating to note that the given end date for this crash is March 31, 1938—the Mars-Uranus conjunction. The financial astrologer might well have advised this as a buying opportunity, as this alignment was close to both a New Moon and to the Nodes moves from Sagittarius into Scorpio. Over and over again we see that it is the combination of planetary events that results in major moves.

1939–1942

The next market crash for us to consider occurred in the opening months of World War II. Between September 1939 and late April 1942, 40.4% value was lost. Given what we have learned so far, we should not be surprised to discover that Chiron was within a degree of 19 Cancer at the start of this period, which concluded at the conjunction of Saturn and Uranus. Note that the latter aspect occurs just every 45 years. Whereas the opposition (1907) brought stress to the marketplace, the conjunction signalled potential for improvement.

Between 1939 and 1942, Pluto made its conjunction with Chiron. Of course financial astrologers would not have known this as the latter was not discovered until 1977. As we have seen though, the phases of this planetary cycle coincides with periods of significant economic difficulty. Their next conjunctions take place in 2069 and 2070.

In September 1939, Saturn moved into Taurus and formed a conjunction with the lunar south Node. Saturn formed this aspect in November 1905, September 1916, and January 1928. Although each of these aspects took place in different signs of the zodiac, on each occasion relative highs were reached.

By 1939, Pluto had moved from Cancer into Leo. Saturn, the faster-moving of the two planets, was about to form a right-angle (square) aspect with that planet. This is a "pruning" aspect when much is cut away and only bare bones left. There is something harsh and austere about this cycle and this aspect especially.

In any cycle two right-angle aspects form: one before and one after the opposition. These are similar to the First and Last quarter phases of the Moon. The 1939 angle was equivalent to the Last Quarter phase: a period of reckoning when all that's occurred since the conjunction is examined and reviewed.

The conjunction that began this cycle took place in the early degrees of Cancer and, geocentrically, formed on three occasions in 1914 and 1915. The previous Last Quarter aspect took place in 1907—coinciding with the panic of that year.

Astro-financiers of the period, having studied those earlier times, might well have concluded that sharp falls would be experienced as the new Saturn-Pluto square formed. Had they also been aware that Chiron was approaching the sensitive 19 Cancer area, they might also have concluded that the September New Moon would be a good opportunity to leave the market.

There was also another square aspect at work: this one between Uranus and Neptune. Recall that the opposition between these two planets coincided with the market losses experienced at the turn of the century. Again it might have been expected that echoes of that earlier time would be heard.

As we now know, markets fell over a period of some 30 months: a duration not dissimilar to that of 1910–13 and of 1931–33. To understand this time frame we should look to the 20-year cycle of Jupiter and Saturn. Thirty months is an eighth of this cycle.

In September 1939, the two planets were 24 degrees apart with Jupiter, the faster moving of the two, moving to form a conjunction with Saturn in early Taurus in 1940. In late April 1942, Jupiter, having moved through Taurus, was at 20 Gemini and again approximately 23 degrees from Saturn. The distance covered from the start to end of this period was roughly 45 degrees.

An investor looking to the planets for guidance as to when to move back into the market might well have come to the conclusion that the optimum time to buy back in would be after the coming Jupiter-Saturn conjunction. They might also have wondered, given that both planets would also form conjunctions with Uranus, if major gains might be made between this conjunction and Jupiter's arrival at 19 Cancer the following year. In this, they would not have been disappointed as indeed, considerable gain was made.

1972–1974

The penultimate period to be considered covers January 1972–74 and embraces both the Vietnam War and Watergate. This period began with Jupiter conjunct the Galactic Center. Recall that Jupiter seems to act as an exaggerator. Alignment with the Galactic Center—even without any other operating factors—has often coincided with a market high. Post this alignment, equity values fell and, by December 1974, had lost 45% value.

The planetary back-drop to this period is Saturn's opposition to Neptune, and Uranus' conjunction with Chiron, and with Neptune at 135 degrees from Chiron. Though again, financial astrologers, still unaware of Chiron's presence could not have factored in two of these aspects, the opposition of Saturn to Neptune, based on those earlier instances of significant negativity, would have suggested economic storms on the horizon.

With the benefit of our relatively recent knowledge of Chiron, its approaching station at 19 Aries (another of the Cardinal signs) in late December 1974, would have alerted the astrologer to the probability of a change of market direction once this degree had been negotiated. The "buy" signals here were the conjunction of Neptune and the Node, Jupiter's right angle to the Node and Chiron's station.

2000–2002

To conclude this chapter and an appraisal of the links between market crashes and planet cycles, we turn to what is now termed the "Dot Com" crash or "Tech Bubble" of the early part of the 21st century.

From January 15, 2000 to October 2002, equities lost 37.8% of value. Of course, by this time, financial astrologers were well aware of the presence of Chiron and its role in earlier periods of difficulty. Its approach to the South Node of the Moon, combined with Saturn's opposition to Pluto and, of course, Pluto's aspect to the Lunar Nodes had many of us on red alert.

During this period, in May 2000, Jupiter and Saturn formed their last conjunction in one of the Earth signs for 240 years. They formed this conjunction with both at almost exact right-angle to Uranus and Neptune. Journalists wondered if the curious planetary formation would result in major incidents, while financial astrologers sensed the high probability of, at the very least a change of market direction and, most likely, a major down-turn. They then were looking for optimum dates for leaving the market.

Investors who left the marketplace on January 15, 2000 left on a high. The planetary picture that day was unusual. The Sun was exactly aligned with Mercury (often a signal for change of trend), and a major stellium (group of planets) formed in Sagittarius. With the Sun applying to the square with Jupiter—and taking into account the looming negative aspects—the astrologer might well have selected this as a date when markets would reach a high, an optimum moment to sell.

As various negative aspects formed, financial astrologers searched for an appropriate date on which to buy back in. That buy signal came on a date after Saturn and the Node had formed their final aspect for the period: a parallel exact in October.

CHAPTER FOUR

ONE DAY GAINS and LOSSES

Of the many myths surrounding the use of financial astrology, a prominent one concerns the identification of particular dates when spectacular gains or losses may—or could have been—made. In this chapter, we will consider the astrology of five top "losses" and five top "gains" trading days in the 20th century. To be precise: those dates on which the open and closing figures showed the greatest percentage of movement. The plan is to see if the planetary configurations in operation, which can be calculated years in advance, would have caught the attention of the astro-investor or trader.

In each case, use will be made of either the opening or closing of trading charts for the day. The two charts have different stories to tell. With the opening of trade chart we see the potential for the day while the close of trade chart describes the final outcome. It is now normal for financial astrologers to observe both charts for each trading day and for each exchange in which they have interest. While this would have been time-consuming for astrologers before the age of the computer, today's financial astrologers can accomplish this task easily and within a matter of minutes.

THE TOP GAINS

Four of the top five examples of gains took place within the space of just a few years. The position of the outer planets is similar in each case. However, as we will see, the dates on which there was maximum activity coincided with faster moving planets, the Sun or Moon, completing a rare planetary picture.

Example 1

On March 15, 1933 the Dow Jones index rose 15.34%. This event followed the Emergency Banking Act that was passed by both

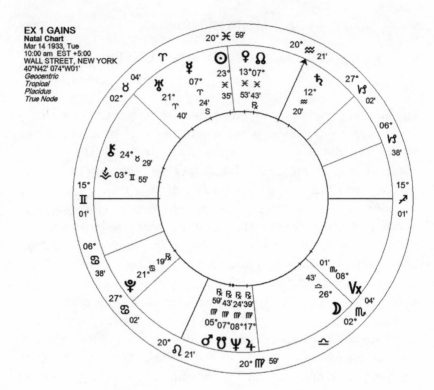

houses of Congress on the evening of March 9th. Wall Street reopened for business on March 15th.

Though not always the case (as we will see in the following examples), it is reasonable to expect that strong aspects from or to Uranus will be marked by unusual moves. Geocentrically, Uranus and Pluto formed five exact squares between 1932 and January 1934. Through this period, the experienced financial astrologer—one who had researched the impact newly discovered Pluto might have had at times of financial stress and strain—would have looked for dates offering a cluster of planetary activity within days of the exact square between Uranus and Pluto. The third of the Uranus-Pluto square aspects occurred on March 8, 1933—coinciding with the triple conjunction of Mars-Neptune and South Node. That same day Venus was moving to oppose Jupiter with both planets square to the Ascendant/Descendant axis as trading began at 10.00am on March 15th.

This day then stood out from others of that period and would no doubt have caught the attention of an astro-trader.

True, Mars, Neptune, and the South Node did not share the same degree position exactly: though astrologers would describe them as being "within orb" of conjunction with one another. (The exact number of degree or "leeway" to be allowed is a matter of some conjecture. Some astrologers allow as much as ten degrees while others use less.) What matters here is that there was a concentration of planets, loosely in conjunction with one another, while Uranus and Pluto were in exact square. The fact that the midpoint of Mars and Neptune was occupied by the lunar south Node added to the potential for this being an eventful day.

So it proved to be. The newly appointed US President, Franklin Roosevelt, determined to bring back confidence to the nation's banking system did so by declaring a four-day banking holiday that shut down the banking system, including the Federal Reserve. In a sense, he manufactured a "cooling off" period (fitting for the Mars-Neptune-South Node conjunction). President Roosevelt may or may not have given thought to the possible impact of chaotic activity on the day of the Full Moon (11th). His decision to demand that a bank holiday be observed perhaps reduced the possibility of that potential chaos. Even so, movement on March 15th was considerable.

The chart for opening of trade on March 15th offers significant instruction for today's financial astrologers:

In 1933, Wall Street opened at 10.00 hours. The Ascendant on that day was 16 Gemini: ruled by Mercury and likely to usher in a day of quick trading. That Jupiter was at nearly exact right angle to this degree underscored the probability of this being a day of super-trading.

We should note too that the asteroid Vesta, often a key feature in charts where financial matters are the focus, was also at near right-angle to Mars. It might be said then that traders were "up and ready" for action. Combined with Jupiter at 17 Virgo, where it conjoined the position of Mars in the chart for the New York Stock Exchange, it likely added to their enthusiasm to do business.

Arguably the most significant astro-feature at this reopening of the banks after the enforced holiday was the Sun and Chiron at exactly a sixth of a cycle apart. This may be viewed as a "correcting" aspect where energy is put in to improving good health. By the end of that trading day it was clear to all that the market was buoyant once more.

Example 2

The next example looks at the closing of trade on October 6, 1931, when gains (14.87%) were only slightly less than seen in Example 1.

When the Ascendant or Midheaven at the start or close of trade changes signs from that on the previous day—this is usually reflected in distinct mood change in the marketplace, resulting, very often, in change of market difection. In this instance it can be seen that the Midheaven at the close was at 2 Sagittarius. It would have been at 1 degree of that sign the day before. It

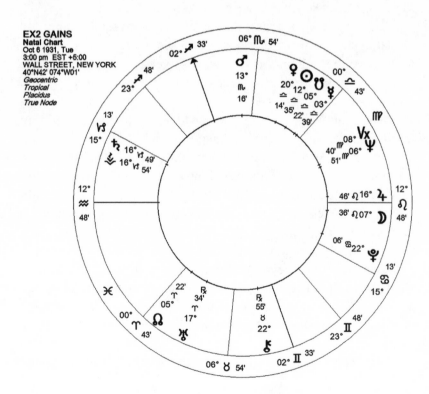

EX2 GAINS
Natal Chart
Oct 6 1931, Tue
3:00 pm EST +5:00
WALL STREET, NEW YORK
40°N42' 074°W01'
Geocentric
Tropical
Placidus
True Node

was on Tuesday 6th, however, when the close of the trading day coincided with the Descendant aligning with the midpoint of the Moon and Jupiter. This planetary picture is associated with "much happiness" and therefore likely to bring significant gain.

On Tuesday 6th, Saturn and Vesta formed a conjunction that itself was exactly 150 degrees from Jupiter. This is a markedly rare configuration. Vesta, closer to the Sun than Saturn, orbits the Sun every 1325 days (every 3.6 years). Thus there is a conjunction of Saturn with Vesta roughly every four years.

Jupiter and Saturn's cycle is approximately 20 years, with the two planets 150 degrees apart both before and after reaching their opposition phase. The angle may also occur more than once depending on the retrograde factor. The point being that the angle between the two does not occur annually; and for it to coincide with an exact Saturn-Vesta conjunction is rare indeed. It should be noted that the same day, Venus was transiting 19 Libra—one of the Cardinal degrees identified as a sensitive degree area and likely to result in a day of singular activity.

Example 3

Gains of over 12% were made on Wednesday, October 30, 1929.

That month was dominated by the conjunction of Chiron with the North Node. What made October 30th stand out was emphasis on 19 degrees of a Cardinal sign coupled with lunar aspects forming during trading hours, and Saturn's position directly at the Midheaven where it conjoined the Galactic Center at close of trade. As may be seen in the chart below, Saturn was also equidistant from the Node and Chiron as well as Vesta. This is a rare planetary picture indeed and indicative of overcoming difficulties and pushing for the top.

Over the Monday and Tuesday (28th and 29th October), the market had been falling.

The financial astrologer would have noted that overnight (29th to 30th October) Mercury would reach the important degree of 19 Libra. The Moon was making its way to that same degree forming a conjunction with Venus and a trine to Jupiter en route.

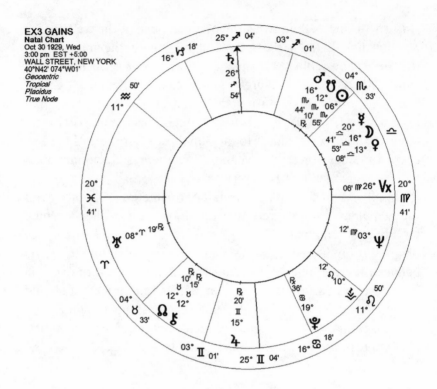

EX3 GAINS
Natal Chart
Oct 30 1929, Wed
3:00 pm EST +5:00
WALL STREET, NEW YORK
40°N42' 074°W01'
Geocentric
Tropical
Placidus
True Node

This planetary picture alone would have been enough for the trader to wonder if a change in market direction would occur.

Example 4

The next chart is for the opening of trade on September 21, 1932. By close of trade, the Dow Jones index had risen 11.36% . Note the presence of Venus at the Midheaven as the opening bell was struck. True, a financial astrologer of the period would have been unaware of Chiron whose existence was unknown until 1977. That said, Venus' position together with Mars' Leo ingress would have been noted along with the exact trine between the Sun and Saturn.

     With our knowledge of Chiron, we see that the planetary positions on September 21, 1932 were exceptional. The Sun was at 28 Virgo, forming an exact Grand Trine with Saturn and

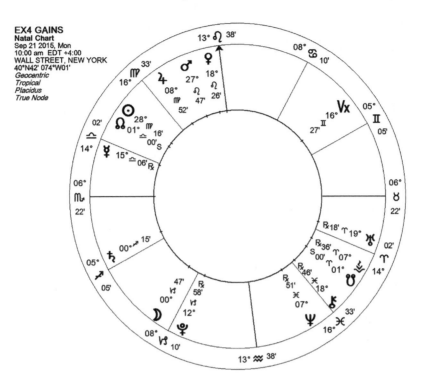

EX4 GAINS
Natal Chart
Sep 21 2015, Mon
10:00 am EDT +4:00
WALL STREET, NEW YORK
40°N42' 074°W01'
Geocentric
Tropical
Placidus
True Node

Chiron. As stated, Mars made its Leo ingress. An ingress usually brings a significant shift in trading behavior. Added to this, we see the Lunar Node at 17 Virgo (the position of Mars in the NYSE chart) while Jupiter came to an exact conjunction with Neptune.

The stage was set for a day of high drama but required the Grand Trine to come into exact formation for this to take place. Had the astro-trader prepared this opening of trade chart, his or her interest would surely have been piqued by the presence of Venus close to the Midheaven.

One final thought about our example chart: the Moon, at 12 Gemini at the opening on Wall Street and at maximum (over 27 degrees) declination would, during the course of the day, be moving toward the North Bending (right angles to the Lunar Nodes at 17 Virgo): yet another signal for strong emotional reaction that might well result in major market movement.

Example 5

The 11.08% rise on Monday, October 13, 2008, comes a close second in terms of percentage rise to Example 4, where gains were 11.36%. The solar position in this chart—20 Libra—is a full degree away from the 19 Cardinal degree area that has been marked in other examples.

It is not the case that there is always large scale movement when the Sun, Moon, Planet, or asteroid crosses 19 degrees of a Cardinal sign. To be reasonably certain that there will be strong movement requires other major configurations to coincide with these degree crossings. The backdrop to the October 2008 move was the conjunction of Chiron with the lunar North Node which, as we have seen in earlier chapters, has marked defining and prominent stock market movements. On October 13, 2008, Chiron and the Node were in square to the Ascendant. That same day, Saturn was 150 degrees from both Chiron and the Node: a rare alignment.

As trading began, the Moon was in exact parallel with Vesta (the trading asteroid) and both were contra-parallel to Uranus: trading would conclude with the Moon in exact opposition to Mercury. This aspect occurs every month of course but rarely occurs as the trading day comes to its close. Those familiar with the works of W. D. Gann will be aware that this coincidence was noted by him with regard to a key trade in cotton.

To summarize:

What is apparent from these five instances is that where Wall Street is concerned, the passage of Mars, Jupiter, and Saturn especially over 17 degrees of Virgo or Pisces is important. With Saturn, a downturn is probable (as we shall see in the next example) though not always the case: much depends on the total planetary-picture. Added to this watch list must be the position of the planets, Sun, Moon, and asteroids at both opening and close of trade. Where these are angular or when aspects are exact, significant movement is probable.

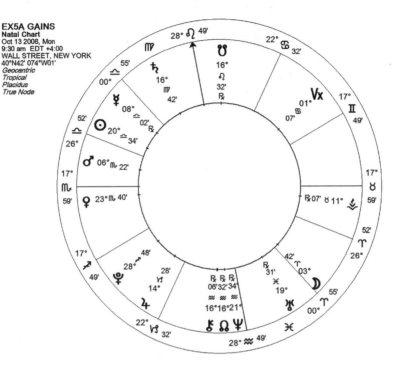

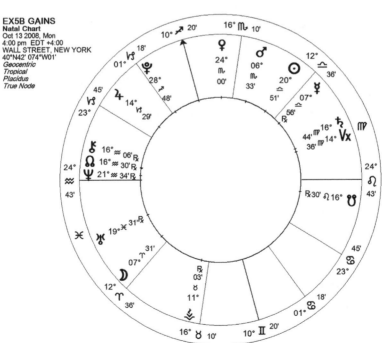

To balance our studies, we consider next the five dates of greatest percentage losses. The relevant dates here are: October 19, 1987 (Example 1); October 28 and 29, 1929 (Example 2); December 18, 1899 (Example 3); November 6, 1929 (Example 4); and August 12, 1932 (Example 5). Respective losses were over 22%, 12%, 11%, 9%, and 8%.

LOSSES

Example 1 Loss

October 19, 1987, was to earn the title "Black Monday" (Australia and New Zealand call this day "Black Tuesday" because of the time zone difference). Stock markets around the world were affected, beginning in Hong Kong, and spreading to Europe, before affecting U.S. markets where stocks lost $503 billion.

Clearly we should expect to see unusual planetary configurations that day. The chart for the opening of trade on Wall Street is shown on the next page.

It is probably no longer necessary to draw attention to the Moon's position at 18 Virgo at a right angle to Saturn at 17 degrees of another Mutable sign and so accentuating a critical degree of the NYSE chart. The fact that it is Saturn and not Jupiter involved in this planetary picture is indicative of harsh realities and potential loss. Certainly the opening of trade chart suggests a gloomy mood. When we expect volatility, we need to understand the whole planetary picture to determine the probable direction.

Technology has been mentioned as a possible "cause" of this crash, so we should look more closely at the position of Uranus in this chart. This planet was in trine to Jupiter—then retrograde—and moving back to form the trine it had made some weeks earlier. This particular aspect relationship is often viewed as being a "good thing." As we saw in an earlier example, this aspect was in force when markets rose substantially.

Yet perhaps the most accurate forecast using this aspect is to suggest that there will be large moves. Where this example of loss differed from the earlier example of gain, was that here Uranus

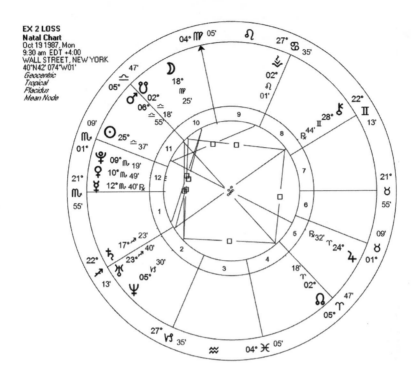

EX 2 LOSS
Natal Chart
Oct 19 1987, Mon
9:30 am EDT +4:00
WALL STREET, NEW YORK
40°N42' 074°W01'
Geocentric
Tropical
Placidus
Mean Node

was "out of bounds": at over 23 degrees of declination. This is where it seems to be at its "wildest": an apt cosmic signature for the abnormal computer trades that took place.

Negative trading began in the markets of the Far East. So we should consider what was happening in the hours prior to Wall Street opening. The Sun would have been in exact opposition to Jupiter while the Moon was moving toward a right-angle with Saturn as markets in the Far East concluded their day.

The chart for the start of trade on Wall Street (above) shows a stellium in Scorpio—with Venus and Pluto within a degree and a half of one another (conjunct) in Scorpio, with both conjunct retrograde Mercury. Those who use opening of trade charts would have noted that this cluster of activity at market opening would be apparent over some days. What singled this date out from other dates was the Moon-Saturn square in those all-important Mutable degrees. Traders would also have noted that Mercury was retrograde, and so would cross back over this degree area

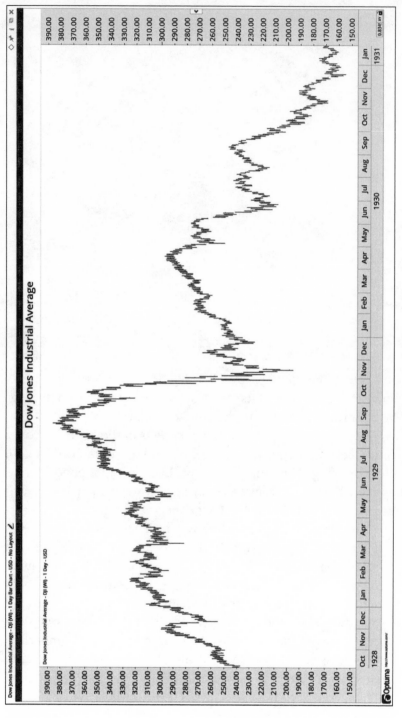

Dow Jones Index November 1928 to January 1930

after reaching its station. The price chart for the Dow Jones Index for this period shows recovery when Mercury returned to this degree after its retrograde period.

Example 2 Loss

October 28 and 29, 1929.

As trading opened on Monday, October 28, 1929, Venus and Uranus, in opposition, lay respectively at the Midheaven and the IC; with Uranus exact on the IC implying instability and unpredictability. The Moon, exactly square the start of trade Ascendant, was at 17 Virgo, and Saturn was conjunct the Galactic Center. The financial astrologer noting this exceptional planetary picture would have been on high alert even without the knowledge that Pluto (not discovered until 1930) was at 19 degrees of a Cardinal sign.

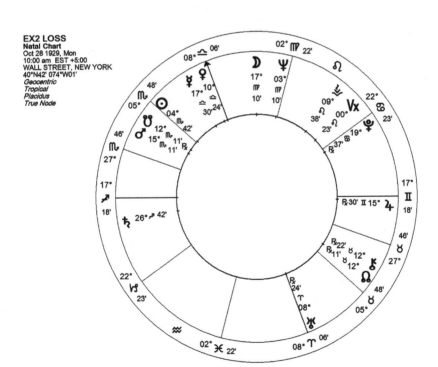

History records that losses continued the following day October 29th: in fact until Mercury had crossed 19 Libra where we now know that it was in its first quarter phase in relation to Pluto (see chart below). This close of trade chart, with Saturn at the Midheaven (as it was for much of that week), shows Venus at the exact midpoint of the Moon and Mercury. Perhaps this indicated that the "balance point" had been reached and that recovery would take place a day later as the Moon moved into conjunction with Mercury—by then leaving the "black hole" area we might associate with 19 Capricorn. The 19 degree area if further accented in that the Ascendant for close of trade that day was at 19 degrees Pisces: so aspecting both Mercury and Pluto making a rare formation and so pointing to a day of singular activity.

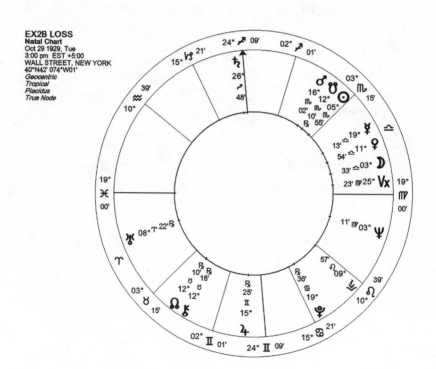

EX2B LOSS
Natal Chart
Oct 29 1929, Tue
3:00 pm EST +5:00
WALL STREET, NEW YORK
40°N42' 074°W01'
Geocentric
Tropical
Placidus
True Node

Example 3 Loss

On Monday, December 18, 1899, the Dow Jones Index fell by 11.99%.

This chart is exceptional: not least because the Midheaven was at 0 Sagittarius, and equidistant from both Vesta and the Moon. The Sun and Saturn are conjoined at 26 Sagittarius—the Galactic Center. Astro-traders would surely have been aware of the development of this planetary picture in the weeks and days ahead of the event.

These traders might also have been concerned that both Venus and Mars were at maximum declination, with the Sun exactly parallel Venus. In considering Venus' position at the all-important 19 Capricorn, they might have made preparation for a difficult day.

The entire planetary picture suggests a day of "fated" trading. Add the Moon's position at 14 Cancer and the knowledge that during trading hours the Moon would be moving toward 19 Cancer

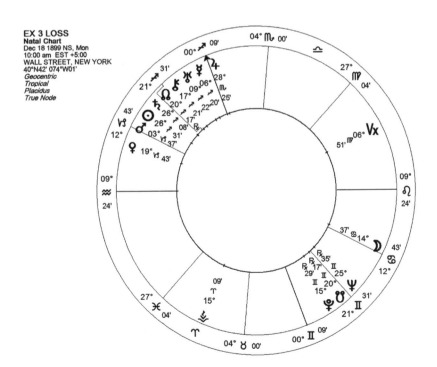

EX 3 LOSS
Natal Chart
Dec 18 1899 NS, Mon
10:00 am EST +5:00
WALL STREET, NEW YORK
40°N42' 074°W01'
Geocentric
Tropical
Placidus
True Node

(though not reaching that degree until after the market closed), and the observant astro-trader would surely have wondered if this would be a day of considerable negative activity.

Example 4 Loss

November 6, 1929

Those who incurred losses in the last days of October 1929 would surely have been pleased to see some recovery in the early days of November. Yet the Dow Jones Index lost almost 10% on November 6th as the Moon moved through Capricorn toward an opposition with Pluto—at 19 Cancer. This aspect coincided with Vesta moving to square the Chiron-Node conjunction, signalling another difficult day that concluded with the Midheaven moving to Capricorn as trading drew to a close.

Saturn, conjunct the Galactic Center is equidistant from both the lunar North Node and from Vesta: another infrequent

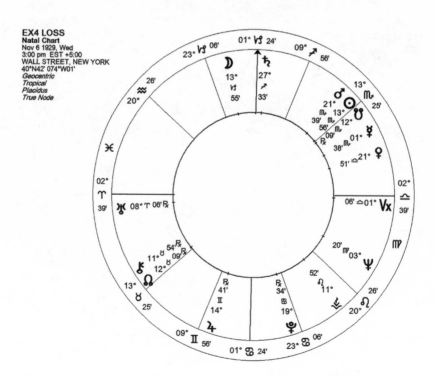

EX4 LOSS
Natal Chart
Nov 6 1929, Wed
3:00 pm EST +5:00
WALL STREET, NEW YORK
40°N42' 074°W01'
Geocentric
Tropical
Placidus
True Node

planetary picture suggesting negative trading. As importantly, Jupiter at the apex of a Yod, lies on the midpoint of the Sun and Moon, indicating that any moves were likely to be great. Not shown on this chart, but also of interest, is that Jupiter was exactly quintile the Ascendant at close of trade: a likely indicator of a major move.

Example 5

August 12, 1932

The Dow Jones Index lost over 8% on August 12, 1932. This chart differs from earlier examples in that there is no emphasis on 19 Capricorn or, indeed, 19 of any of the Cardinal signs. However, the lunar South Node was at 17 Virgo where it aligns with Mars' position in the NYSE chart.

At the opening bell on Wall Street both Venus and Mars were at the Midheaven: a rare occurrence. Jupiter had just made its Virgo ingress with Saturn, its Aquarius ingress, so that the two planets were in exact 150 degree (critical phase) aspect.

Experienced astro-traders know that as Jupiter changes signs (as it does every year) there is commonly a sharp reaction in the marketplace. On this occasion, with Vesta leaving a conjunction with Chiron and shortly making a square aspect to Jupiter and a trine to Saturn, a significant day would be forecast.

During the course of the day, the Moon moved through the early degrees of Capricorn to conclude the trading day exactly opposite the midpoint of the Venus/Mars conjunction—further evidence, if needed, that this would be a day of negative trading.

The importance of aspects that take place either at market opening, or at closing, cannot be over-stated. These offer a statement of intent (with regard to the opening chart) and of delivery at the end of the day. Setting a computer program to run through open and close of market charts is a rewarding exercise—as often this will identify key trading days.

It is not necessary for a planet to be angular (i.e. exact on the Ascendant, Descendant, MC or IC) in either the opening or closing chart for a trading day to stand out. Just as revealing may

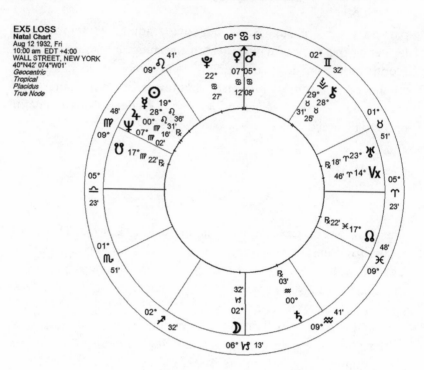

be an exact aspect made by the Moon in one trading center but not in another. For example, the Sydney, Australia, markets might close with an exact Moon-Saturn conjunction that is not at work in other markets. Quite simply because the Moon moves at a rate of 12–14 degrees per day, and so, by the time the next market opens, the aspect may no longer be exact.

CONCLUSION

The examples offered covered days of extraordinarily dramatic market activity. Key factors were:

1. Planets or the Moon placed at 19 degrees of the Cardinal signs
2. Planets placed at 17–18 degrees Virgo (where they align with Mars in the natal chart for the NYSE)
3. An ingress (where a planet enters a new sign)
4. Chiron-Node aspects

5. Conjunctions to any of the four angles of the chart at either open or close of trade.
6. Prominently positioned asteroids Vesta and Ceres
7. Planets at extreme declination (out of bounds)

Note that it is not one of these factors alone that marks a significant date, but three or more of these factors at work simultaneously. Today's computer software permits the user to animate the chart for a specific time and to scroll through weeks, months or years noting when planets come to exact alignments with chart angles. This exercise, which can, of course, be done with the charts for opening and closing of trade, has proved a valuable exercise since I began to use this system a few years ago.

CHAPTER FIVE

RECESSIONS, CONSTRUCTION, LAND AND PROPERTY CYCLES

Nowhere are the rhythms of boom and bust more evident than in the property market. Compelling work has been done by the researchers and financial analysts Fred Harrison (author of *Boom, Bust, House Prices, Banking and Depression of 2010*) and Phillip J. Anderson (author of *The Secret Life of Real Estate and Banking*) who identified a pulse of approximately 18 years: almost coinciding with the lunar nodal cycle of 18.6 years. Like a heavy base drum beat, property boom is followed by a crash. Over and above the 18 year pulse, intricate rhythms are played: arguably defined by shorter planet cycles. Phil Anderson concluded that at least in Western economies, a property clock is at work.

This chapter focuses on the syncopation between land prices, construction, and business cycles with the movement of the planets as they orbit the Sun and concludes with a brief study of property cycles in a few key cities and a case-study.

It might be supposed that the acknowledged 18-plus-year property cycle as uncovered by Harrison and Anderson could also be divided into four even parts—much as is done with the Sun-Moon cycle which divides into New, First Quarter, Full and Last Quarter lunar phase. That can be done. However, the interaction of this 18-year cycle with the cycles of Mars with Vesta, and Jupiter with Saturn, results in syncopation. Diving a cycle into four quarters is, of course, only the base rhythm. Other rhythms react with it. Anderson, who makes much use of a property clock acknowledges that there is a variation of the length of each "hour" of his clock. It may be that this is due to the interaction of different planet cycles whose lengths are very different. Harrison and Anderson came to the conclusion that the apparent 18-year cycle could be divided into two parts: one which brought a 14-year upswing in prices and four years which brought lows, house price collapse and depression.

RECESSIONS

Property prices are, of course, affected by recessions. Before looking more closely at the proposed 18-year real estate cycle from
the planet-cycle perspective, it is worth reviewing the primary
recessions affecting the West through the last quarter millennium. True: some sources give different dates for recessions and
there are different ways to define the start and end of a recession,
depending on the way the definition is used, and to some extent
the dates for one country differ from those of another. Yet it is
possible to discern an over-arching series of primary recessions
affecting the West in particular. The dates of these primary recessions are given below. A clear pattern emerges:

1776, 1794, 1812, 1830, 1848, 1866, 1884,
1902, 1920, 1938, 1956, 1974, 1992 and 2010

Each is separated by 18 years.

Economists have long-noted that each recession differs
in nature from earlier ones. This is, to the student of planetary
cycles, entirely understandable as the positions of the planets
during each of these years will differ greatly from those of earlier
or subsequent ones.

Even so, it is compelling to consider the position of the lunar
North Node during each of these years given that this cycle length
is 18.6 years. Of course, if recessions were exactly this length
apart, then the list of years given above would be quite different.
Clearly something "happens" to cause a "slip" of a little more
than 6 months. The lunar north Node passes through the signs
at a regular pace. However, each cycle takes place against the
backdrop of very different planetary positions.

Close study of the years listed above reveals an interesting
sequence when the sign position of Jupiter—which moves though
the signs every 11.88 years—is taken into account, along with the
lunar nodal position.

In the following table the first column gives the years of
the recessions. In the second column we have the sign which
the Node is transiting. The Node travels backwards through the

zodiac i.e. in the order of Pisces, Aquarius, Capricorn, Sagittarius, Scorpio etc. Yet this list shows the Node to be moving against this rhythm—moving the "regular" way through the signs i.e. Aries followed by Taurus, Gemini, Cancer, Leo, Virgo etc. Note too that the Node is, with just one exception, in a sign twice before moving on to the next.

RECESSION	NODAL SIGN	JUPITER
1776	Leo	Cancer
1794	Leo	Capricorn
1812	Virgo	Cancer
1830	Virgo	Capricorn
1848	Virgo/Libra	Cancer
1866	Libra	Aquarius and Capricorn
1884	Libra	Cancer /Leo/Virgo
1902	Scorpio	Capricorn/Aquarius
1920	Scorpio	Leo/Virgo
1938	Sagittarius/Scorpio	Aquarius
1956	Sagittarius	Leo/Virgo
1974	Sagittarius	Aquarius/Pisces
1992	Capricorn	Virgo/Libra
2010	Capricorn	Pisces

Assuming that the 18 year pattern continues, we might reasonably draw the conclusion that the next recession will take place in 2028. Noting the sequence of nodal positions by sign, we would require the Node to then be in either Capricorn or Aquarius. The lunar north Node moves into Aquarius in July 2026 and crosses into Capricorn in March 2028: exactly as we would anticipate if the sequence were to continue.

Next we turn to the last column which gives Jupiter's position by sign. Again a pattern emerges: throughout the latter part of the 18th and through the 19th centuries, Jupiter alternated between the signs of Cancer and Capricorn.

Toward the end of the 19th century, the pattern adjusted: this time putting emphasis on the signs following Cancer and

Capricorn: those of Leo and Aquarius. Then, in 1974, the next pair of signs were involved: Virgo and Pisces.

Using this sequence, we should expect the next recession to occur when Jupiter is in Virgo or Libra. Jupiter moves into Virgo in July 2027, reaching Libra the following year. If our forecast based on the Lunar Node position for a primary recession in 2027–28 is correct, then Jupiter is exactly where we would expect it to be for the sequence to continue.

For investors to make use of this potentially valuable information however, they also need to identify the boom years. As noted at the start of this chapter, those who have made a study of property cycles using non-astrological methods describe the 18-year cycle as being broken into two distinct but unequal parts. The first part is long: approximately 14 years, with a shorter "boom" period of approximately four years preceding recession. If the projected recession of 2027–28 is correct, then a four year boom phase ought to take place between (approximately) 2023 and 2027. It is, of course, only 13 years between the recession of 2010 and 2023: a year short of the 14-year sub-division of the 18-year cycle. Yet it may be that the boom years will take place between 2024 and 2028: a certain license must be allowed.

Within the 14-year period (the most recent beginning in 2010), minor rhythms operate. It takes a couple of years to move out of recession. There is then a noticeable cessation of prices falling and, at least within the cycle beginning in 2010, stabilization before an increase in property prices. Indeed, recognizable recovery (at least in major cities) was apparent from 2012 and may have been marked by the opposition of Mars to Vesta (a four-year cycle). Through 2013, 2014, and 2015, house prices rose though not in all areas.

At the opposition of Mars to Vesta in late 2016, a downturn is likely and may be most apparent in the capital cities where prices have risen markedly. A downturn in these areas could last through to 2022–23 and be led by the forecasted global financial crisis of 2017 (as Saturn moves across the Galactic Center and as Pluto reaches the sensitive degree of 19 Capricorn). We should note too that Jupiter arrives at its square with Pluto that same year: an aspect that often coincides with financial stress.

While it is true that some economic historians find parallels between one recession and another, they would agree that there are differences. Time and the planets move on—so that each recession is driven by human desires that are peculiar to the years involved. We can surely all accept that the booms and busts of one century will differ from those of another: for instance, the property booms and busts experienced (and driven by) the post-WW II "baby boomers" are not at all the same as those experienced by people who lived through the greater part of the 19th century.

The next boom period, if it does arrive "on cue" around 2023–24, will no doubt be driven by reasons that are quite different to those of a quarter, half, or even whole century earlier.

Analysis of charts for around the period of the February 2026 Mars-Vesta conjunction shows Jupiter in Cancer in positive (trine) aspect to the Node. It may be that prices move fast that month: perhaps the optimum period for some people to sell with a view to enjoying possible low prices in the expected recession of 2028.

LAND PRICES

The table of peak land values given on page 89 yields another interesting planetary "pattern." With the exception of 1973, land prices have peaked approximately three to six years after each recession. If the above forecast holds true, then these prices should peak again a few years after the expected recession of 2027–28: in the early years of the 2030s. These would arguably be the optimum years for selling land bought, perhaps, at low price some years earlier.

The land price peak value table covering almost two hundred years has a few entries on which to focus our research. We might consider the Mars-Vesta conjunction immediately prior to the year listed. In 1850 and 2002 (respectively before the high land prices of 1854 and 2006) Mars and Vesta conjoined in Cancer: a sign considered to give above average attention to "nesting" and ownership. Astrologers would not be surprised to see evidence of a land price increase following conjunctions in this sign. The next conjunction of Mars and Vesta in Cancer occurs in 2053.

There is a conjunction of Mars and Vesta in Sagittarius (2018): similar to the conjunction prior to the recession of 1866. It may be that 2018 will mark the start of another minor boom in land prices. This minor boom is likely to be surpassed by the major boom which should—according to our theory—take place in the early 2030s.

What is clear from study of the Mars-Vesta cycle including the first quarter, opposition and last quarter of its phases is that there is above average emphasis on phases accenting the Mutable (Gemini, Virgo, Pisces and Sagittarius) signs. Years containing such aspects in any of these signs have, in the past, witnessed a rise in land value. That then suggests the potential for sharp land price rises through 2021–24 when many phases accent these signs.

The Mars-Vesta conjunction of 2022 may well mark the start of the next property "boom." It may be that this is led by rising land values from 2021, in turn suggesting that investing in land prior to 2021 could be a positive investment move.

As is obvious from this table, there is no regularity, but an apparent "pulse" of 18 years. Consideration must be given to the years which did not adhere to the 18-year rule: the gap between 1925 and 1973 is considerable. This 48-year interval is not a multiple of 18 years—though, as we shall see, the pulse may well have been dormant through this period.

The Great 18-Year Real Estate Cycle					
Peaks in Land Value Cycle	Interval (years)	Peaks in Construction Cycle	Interval (years)	Peaks in Business Cycle	Interval (years)
1818	–	–	–	1819	–
1836	18	1836	–	1837	18
1854	18	1856	20	1857	20
1872	18	1871	15	1873	16
1890	18	1892	21	1893	20
1907	17	1909	17	1918	25
1925	18	1925	16	1929	11
1973	48	1972	47	1973	44
1979	6	1978	6	1980	7
1989	10	1986	8	1990	10
2006	17	2006	20	December 2007	18

Data source: Fred E. Foldvary *The Depression of 2008.*
The Gutenberg Press, 2007.

It would be rare indeed for only one planetary cycle to have effect on an index, property cycle, or equity. It is often the case that although there are clear indicators of one relevant cycle, other cycles "interfere" or work with the identified major cycle. This study of land values offers an excellent example of how an aspect between the Lunar Node and a slow moving planet disrupts the major pulse.

In the years listed, the Lunar Node was positioned as follows: 1836–Taurus; 1854–Taurus; 1872–Gemini; 1890–Gemini; 1907–Cancer; 1925–Leo/Cancer; 1973–Capricorn; 1979–Virgo; 1989–Aquarius; 2006–Pisces.

Through the 19th century, the Node was in the same sign twice before moving on into the next sign using the normal sequence (recall, the Lunar Node moves backwards through the signs). The rhythm was clearly broken after 1925. Had it continued, we would have expected the Node to have its second visit to Cancer (roughly 1924), followed 18 years later in 1942 and 1960 by the Node's presence in Leo, before reached Virgo in the 1970s. Though the rhythm was broken, the sound of that distant drum beat becomes audible again in 1979.

Had that beat continued from 1925, we would have expected land values to be at a high 18 years later in 1943. The fact that this year is not listed perhaps says something about the disruption caused by the World War of that period. Assuming that 1943 had indeed brought high land values, this should have happened again 18 years later when the Node was in Leo in 1961. This ought then to have been followed by two Virgo Node series 18.6 and 37.2 years later i.e. 1979 and 1998. As we see, land prices were indeed high in 1979 as the Node moved through Virgo but the next year in the expected sequence (1997) is not mentioned. In fact, the final two entries in the table: 1989 and 2006 most definitely deviated from the initially-identified sequence.

A syncopated rhythm—or aspects made between a planet and the Node—may be at work. The out-of-synch years are 1973, 1989, and 2006. These years have one major astro-key in common: in each of those years, slow-moving Pluto formed a square aspect to the Lunar Node. It is entirely possible that this is a new rhythm—developed after the most recent conjunction of Uranus and Pluto in 1966—which will gain prominence through the 21st century.

If this were to be the case, then a sequence of two Virgo Nodes (separated by approximately 18 years) would be followed by two years sharing Node positions in Libra: 1995–97 and 2014–16. At the time of writing, the latter seems to be at work. In London and in many other capital cities, prices are high. That being the case we may wonder if prices will be high again when the Node passes through the next sign of the sequence, Scorpio, in 2031/32.

If this proves to be the case, then we should expect high land prices in 2023, 2036, 2040, and 2049—this latter neatly coinciding with the other rhythm that suggests high land prices at the half-way point of the 21st century.

In April 2019, Pluto aligns with the South Lunar Node and in Capricorn. This could disrupt the next sequence

CONSTRUCTION CYCLE

The construction cycle, as given in the above table, responds to another and very important planet cycle. First though, note that there is a difference of between one and three years with high land values.

Construction requires ideas and architects, planning permission and managers, followed by materials and builders—and funding. It should, perhaps, come as no surprise that there is evidence of this cycle correlating with different phases in the Jupiter-Saturn cycle.

In 1836, the first of the key years given, construction increased as Jupiter moved through Leo and Saturn through Scorpio, the planets then arriving at their Last Quarter phase. Similarly, in 1854, the two planets were respectively in Aries and Cancer— once again at right-angles and in their Last Quarter phase.

We might reasonable have expected that the next year in the sequence would be in 1875–76 when the two planets would once again be in square to one another and in their Last Quarter phase.

Yet the next year given in this table is four years earlier, in 1871. That year, Jupiter, in Cancer with the Lunar Node, was in opposition phase to Saturn, in Capricorn. The fact that once again "hard" aspects between Jupiter and Saturn were involved should come as no great surprise.

In 1925, the next year listed in the table, Jupiter was at the south Node. The connection with this axis seems important. Jupiter formed a conjunction with the North Node in 1972—the next year listed.

An interval of just six years separates the construction peak of 1972 and the next year in the table, 1978. That year Jupiter, in Cancer made a square with the Node. It may be that aspects between Jupiter and the Nodes moving through the Cardinal signs, but especially Cancer or Capricorn, prompts a surge in activity while Saturn in similar aspect coincides with a slow-down.

In 1986 and 2006 peaks in the construction cycle coincided with Jupiter in square to Saturn.

What may be of particular interest to the beginning student is that the years when the two planets have formed a conjunction are not listed. Of course it may be that it is during this period that the idea for a construction project is formed and the process begins. It would appear however that peak activity coincides with years when Jupiter and Saturn are either in square or opposition to one another, or when Jupiter forms a square to the Lunar Node.

Now, in the second half of the second decade of the 21st century, Jupiter and Saturn are moving toward their 2020 conjunction. In 2017, Jupiter will square the Nodes and yes, it is possible that there will be a flurry of activity that year. We should however expect to see a decline in construction through 2019 and 2020 with recovery in 2023 when Jupiter conjoins the Node, and through 2024 when the two planets are once again in square.

LOCAL PROPERTY PRICES, HOME SALES AND PURCHASES

We should not be surprised that there is so much variation in prices between one geographical area and another: some areas are simply more desirable than others. While it is possible to give generalizations—as above—local values often appear to buck prevailing trends.

It is often possible to obtain a horoscope for the founding of a city or town and not uncommon for the rise and fall of local prices to coincide with progression and transits to that chart. While this is a valuable astro-technique, another technique is also of value:

Geodetics assumes an Earth zodiac which, though in theory could begin at any point on Earth, is most commonly based on Greenwich, London. In this system, the Midheaven at Greenwich is given the value of 0 Aries and each degree of longitude—moving eastward—represents each subsequent degree of the zodiac. The simplicity of this system facilitates research.

Using Greenwich Geodetics, Berlin at 13 degrees longitude would have a Midheaven of 13 Aries, while Central London, just a degree west of Greenwich, has a Midheaven of 29 Pisces and Hong Kong, at 114 East, would have a Midheaven of 24 Cancer.

It appears that the most important factor influencing house prices are nodal transits to the Ascendant and Midheaven geodetic degrees of a city. When conjunctions to these points coincide with aspects made by outer planets, the effect is marked. In recent years, London property prices have escalated. It could even be argued that London property has become another world currency.

Central London has a Geodetic Midheaven of 29 Pisces, and an Ascendant of 26 Cancer. Clearly there are other towns (sharing the same longitude as London) that share this Midheaven position. Once their latitude is taken into account, the Ascendant varies slightly. This, coupled with their non-capital status could go some way toward explaining why house price values have varied enormously throughout the UK.

While house prices in some areas have risen dramatically, other areas have witnessed the opposite: many cannot sell their home despite having dropped the price. Indeed, there are some properties in the UK offered at just a tenth of the price of average properties in London. Some areas have been particularly badly affected, with house prices not rising as in London, but falling again and again. Belfast for example has a Geodetic Midheaven of 23 Pisces and Ascendant of 25 Cancer: apparently not so dissimilar to that of London. Tempting as it might then be to dismiss this technique, when the position of Fixed Stars and the Galactic Center are taken into account, it is not so difficult to see why one area benefits and another is challenged. Very few cities in the United Kingdom lie east of Greenwich: a good example is Ipswich with a geodetic Midheaven of 1 Aries. The Ascendant degree remains in Cancer however and accents the influence of the Moon (from these Cancer Ascendants).

The Moon waxes and wanes as do house prices. What seems particularly important is the position of the Lunar Node as it transits the geodetic charts of the various cities together with the position of the outer planets.

Those who bought London properties in early 2010 as Uranus reached London's geodetic Midheaven will surely not have been disappointed. The value of these homes has risen sharply. Not long after Uranus reached this point and apparently kick-started this trend, the Lunar Node aligned with the Geodetic Descendant for London. The rate of growth increased as the Node moved through Sagittarius (foreign buyers), and Scorpio (bringing speculators), and accelerated even further as the Node crossed into Libra (often manifesting in second-home purchases for investment). With Jupiter joining the Node in Virgo as it opposed the Geodetic MC, prices soared. The next cyclical low should be expected in 2028—which concurs with the earlier study of the Node-Jupiter positions by sign given earlier in this chapter.

New York City too has seen a substantial increase in real estate prices in recent years. New York is west of Greenwich and has a geodetic Midheaven of 14 Capricorn. The Ascendant is 27 Leo. Through 2014–15, the two planets Uranus (by square) and Pluto (by conjunction), coupled with a lunar eclipse at right-angles to this degree, affected this important axis: suggesting a shake-up in local house prices with the potential for prices to reach a high as proved to be the case.

The key degrees for Hong Kong give a Midheaven of 22 Cancer and Ascendant of 22 Libra: thus the transiting nodal axis affects Hong Kong at quite different periods to those of London or New York.

In 2020, Pluto will reach 22 Capricorn (the IC of Hong Kong's geodetic chart) while the nodal axis also affects the chart. It is probable that this period will mark the beginning of a four-year decline in Hong Kong real estate prices.

Geodetic charts can be created for any location and generally provide fascinating study. They can be considered alongside the dates of incorporation of cities and municipalities. Property investors find such studies to be valuable.

At a more obvious level however, for those wishing to sell their home, it is attention to their progressed charts alongside transits to their personal charts—and, to the chart of the date of purchase of their present home, that are more likely to be used to determine optimum times to put their property on the market.

While only part of the story, attention should be given to the position of the transiting Nodes through these charts and also to transiting Mercury's position. Mercury in good aspect to the Ascendant is often a signal for a change of environment and a house sale.

One of the best indicators of significant general asset management (often resulting in change of residence) is the progressed Moon's declination cycle. The creation of this chart is of great assistance even when the actual time of birth is only loosely known. Whereas the position of the Moon changes by approximately one degree every two hours, the Moon's declination moves at less than four degrees per day: making the Moon's declination less sensitive to uncertainty in the time of birth.

It is common to create this graph to cover as much as 90 years (representing the lifespan) and to make enquiry of the client as to what their circumstances were at the turning points on the graph and when the curved line crossed 0 degrees.

Though study of this progressed Moon in declination chart is most useful, it would be quite wrong to suggest that people move only when lunar lines are crossed or when the turning points of these curves are reached. It is perhaps more accurate to say that at these junctures individuals review resources (often as a result of a change in circumstances), and that there is subsequent change of attitude to both financial matters and to application of talent. Indeed, some people change career at these points choosing these periods to explore natural gifts.

Another method of determining house sale, move, or purchase concerns the natal Ascendant and IC positions. The gap between Jupiter's crossing of the natal IC and its eventual arrival at the progressed IC can be swiftly estimated. The progressed MC/IC axis moves at approximately one degree per year. It then might take someone in their sixties a couple of years (Jupiter moving at a rate of approximately 30 degrees per year) to finally complete a sale or purchase.

To be clear, it is not always possible for an individual to take advantage of the overall property cycle. Individual needs may be such that property sale and purchase has to be made at what might be considered as less than favorable times.

In such instances, the natal and progressed charts are taken into consideration using some of the techniques listed above.

CHAPTER SIX

CURRENCIES AND CURRENCY FORECASTS

A few foreign exchange dealers have a particular interest in the position of the Moon and planets; observing some striking parallels between turning points during the trading day and particular alignments. Their frustration when discovered planetary configurations do not work consistently is understandable: much more research is necessary. But even so there is compelling evidence of a link between planetary and lunar positions and the highs and lows of trading days. Before looking at one or two of the techniques these individuals employ, we will first look to see what can be gained from studying the known charts or horoscopes of the Euro and US dollar.

There are over a hundred currencies in operation around the globe, although most are not actively traded, and a whole book could—and should—be given over to the study of these and the fluctuations in their value against other currencies. This chapter can only offer a cursory overview. The aim here is to introduce charts that are worthy of the reader's further study and an explanation of some of the techniques employed by Astro-Forex traders.

EURO

Currencies are ever-evolving. Some have lasted hundreds of years, others for just a fraction of that time. It is rare for the actual launch date and time of a currency to be known—but that is the case with the Euro. True, there are many charts for the Euro that could be studied as countries have adopted the currency at different times. Each of these dates has import. It could be argued that the date, time, and place of the agreement that the single currency should be put in place is significant. That, though, would be the chart for the idea not for the tangible currency itself.

The following chart is for the launch of the actual physical

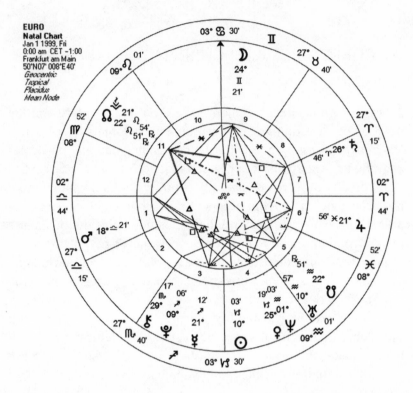

currency. It is set for midnight, local time in Frankfurt, Germany on January 1, 1999. It marks an extraordinary planetary signature (horoscope). Research to date reveals that aspects to this chart have reflected many of the Euro's ups and downs. The chart for Frankfurt is the dominant chart—as it was the celebrations at midnight from that financial market that were televised and beamed across the European Union, and regarded as "the moment." As of that date millions of people—not just traders—were interested in its value and its fluctuations against other currencies.

While this chart is in common use, no less important are the charts for that same date and time but set for the various capitals of the countries that adopted the currency. As we shall see, when this chart is set for either Nicosia, capital of Cyprus or Athens, capital of Greece, we can understand better why those countries have experienced the financial strains of recent years.

Those new to astrology should not be put off by the following short analysis of this chart as primarily we will focus on the clear geometric shapes contained within it. One of these is highly unusual: a kite formation made up of an apparent equilateral triangle between the Node, Saturn and Mercury with the Moon, at the apex of another triangle directly opposite Mercury.

So-called kite formations do not occur every day and were recognized by the ancients as bringing eventful-ness. There is little doubt that the Euro has been subjected to moments of high drama since its launch. At one point, as the Euro was going through a particularly torrid time, the retired President of the European Union stated that at the time of its launch key members of the Union had been "flying a kite" and had little idea where the wind would take them. How appropriate!

In this chart the Sun is in Capricorn. Just as we might deduce if this were the chart of an individual, the astrologer draws the conclusion from this factor alone that the Euro wants to be a "main" player. An exact quintile (fifth of a circle) between the Sun and Jupiter indicates the Euro needs to be a "star." A further sign of "special-ness" can be seen by the kite formation with one small triangle, whose apex is the Moon in Gemini, on top of a large triangle formed by Mercury (opposite the Moon) at close to 120 degrees from the North Node and from Saturn.

The opposition between the Moon and Mercury occurs every month and is in place (allowing for orb) for a period of a few hours. The Moon is said to describe the people and their emotions while Mercury is the planet of commerce. It is perhaps understandable that many have a love-hate relationship with this particular currency.

The Ascendant for Frankfurt is 2 degrees Libra. In Athens the rising (Ascendant) degree is 15 degrees of that sign and places the Midheaven at 17 Cancer—a near exact right angle. Thus it was that as Uranus and Pluto, also at right angles between 2010 and 2015, aligned with these degrees that financial pressure was felt acutely in first Cyprus, then Athens. The Cyprus crisis.

In the chart calculated for Frankfurt, Mars is apparently a full 16 degrees from the Ascendant whereas in Athens Mars is just two degrees from the Ascendant. Mars' position usually tells a story about a fight. Astrologers observe the motion of the planets each day and make notes as to those periods when slow moving planets will align with the sensitive points of a chart. As Uranus opposed the Ascendant degree for Athens in 2015, the Greek government determined that it would not adhere to the rules of the Euro club.

In the Euro's chart (and whichever European capital the chart is set for) Pluto, the slowest moving of the planets lies at 9 degrees of Sagittarius. Pluto moved into the next sign, Capricorn, in 2008. An earlier chapter showed how this ingress coincided with the recent global financial crisis. As Pluto made its way toward the Sun's position in the Euro's chart, there was much discussion as to whether the currency would survive being buffeted by the fierce financial currents in operation at the turn of that decade.

The solar position in any chart may be described as the "life force." In the chart of a company or political entity, it describes the head of the organization. As Pluto moved toward this degree, the position held by the various heads of government making up the European community and, specifically, the position held by the President of the European Bank, was an unenviable one. We may never know just how many power (Pluto) struggles took place between 2010 and 2013 as Pluto edged ever closer to the Sun's position.

The struggle for the Euro to survive is unlikely to be over. Pluto has yet to cross the base of the Frankfurt chart at 17 Capricorn (2016-18) form a square to Saturn (end of the decade) and, over a decade later, pass the position of the progressed Sun (2032).

This relatively long-term view will surely be of interest to investors in the Euro region. Indeed, it could be argued that between 2016 and 2020 would be an optimum time to buy into this currency whose value may well increase in the next decade before it experiences difficulties again (from 2029–32) as Pluto nears the progressed Sun position.

Forex traders tend to be less interested in this long range forecast and far more interested in medium and short term trading. Several have commented on the link between angles formed in the Mars-Vesta cycle and key turning points in the

EUR-USD exchange rate. That these bodies of the solar system should be involved is perhaps understandable given the positions of both Mars and Vesta in the 1999 chart. In that chart, Vesta (the trading asteroid) is conjunct the North Node (and this will be the case whichever European capital is used for calculation), while Mars is close to the horizon in this same chart (just how close being dependent on the city for which the chart is calculated). It is noteworthy also that Vesta was in close contra-parallel with Uranus in the 1999 chart: suggesting the potential for a pattern of volatile trading that could be exaggerated when the Moon passes either position.

For the moment we will focus on the fact that Mars is close to the Ascendant in the various charts. Mars moves through all twelve signs of the zodiac every 780 days. In astrological terms Mars is not the "ruler" of the Euro chart: our attention is drawn by virtue of its position somewhere near the Ascendant (all dependent on the location used). It seems then that there is a Martian quality to the Euro: some might even describe it as a "little fighter."

The importance of Mars in relation to the Euro is confirmed when a study is made of the Euro's value against the USD. When Mars transits either Aries or Scorpio (the signs in which it is said to work best), there is marked activity in the rate of exchange.

A common trading technique is to compare conditions at particular highs or lows. It was observed at two recent "lows," that there were exactly 779 days between them—an almost exact Mars cycle. Research is now being carried out to explore the half-way and other fractions of this cycle to determine if these dates yield clues as to minor turning points in trading. The results are tantalizing and may work beyond the EUR-USD relationship to other currency pairings.

It should be expected then that the Euro might also march to a Saturn rhythm, as Saturn is the planet most associated with the Capricorn Sun position in this Euro chart. One possibility is to review the effect of Saturn through the various signs, remembering of course that a complete Saturn cycle is almost three decades in length, and that the Euro's physical form has only been in

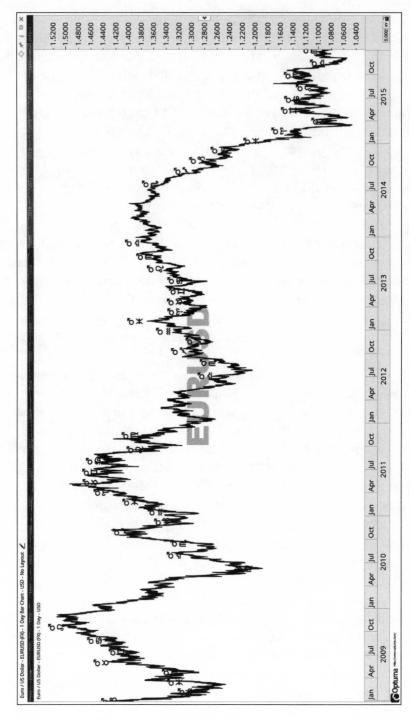

EURUSD 2009–2015 with Mars by Sign (Geocentric)

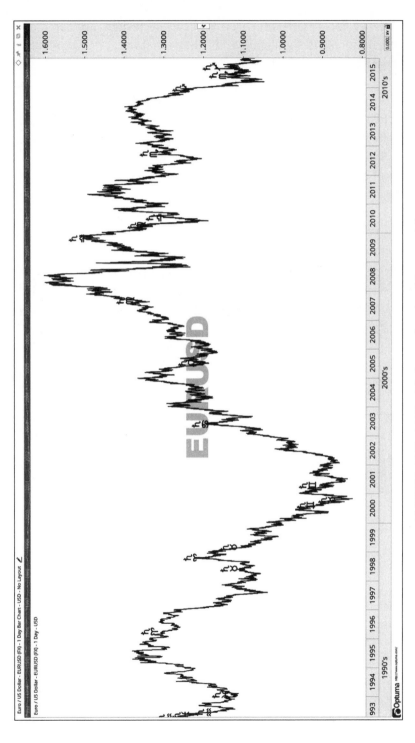

EURUSD 1993–2015 with Saturn by sign (Geocentric)

existence for a half-Saturn cycle. Even so it does appear that a Saturn ingress is significant as is shown below:

At its lowest, in 2001, a Euro bought just 0.90 USD. At this time Saturn had just arrived in the sign of Gemini. A little over seven years later in 2008, Saturn arrived at 0 Virgo—the next in sequence of the Mutable signs—and one Euro bought USD 1.6: a rate to which it has yet to return. If a Mutable sign ingress by Saturn does indeed say something about change of pace, if not of actual direction, then it would be reasonable to anticipate another important price point to be reached as Saturn moved to the next Mutable sign, Sagittarius.

From the geocentric perspective, and thanks to retrograde motion, Saturn made two Sagittarius ingresses: on December 24, 2014 and September 18, 2015. This latter date also happened to be a solar eclipse, suggesting that of the two dates, it might be the more important. Between December 2014 and September 2015, the Euro reached lows of 1.06 USD. Note that the Euro did not fall to its "Virgo" low, but that the general direction as Saturn moved from Virgo to Sagittarius was downward. It seems reasonable to expect that the next phase of this particular Saturn cycle, as Saturn moves from Sagittarius to Pisces, will see the Euro's value increase until it reaches another turning point in 2025 when Saturn makes its Pisces ingress. That said, 2015–25 is unlikely to see steady and incremental increase of Euro value against the USD, as considerable pressure on EUR value is likely to be experienced in 2017 and 2018.

In the horoscope for the Euro, Mercury and Jupiter are at 21 degrees of Sagittarius and Pisces respectively, while the Moon is at 24 Gemini, Venus at 25 Capricorn, Saturn at 26 Aries, and Chiron at 29 Scorpio. As transiting planets move between 21 and 29 degrees of any sign, the planet concerned may be said to activate the Euro's chart—most likely giving rise to considerable volatility.

Through the latter part of 2014, Saturn was in Scorpio and moving from through 21 to 29 degrees of that sign. Through those months the value of the Euro against the USD fell substantially. A tuning point was reached as Saturn finally passed on into

Sagittarius (and so reached 0 degrees of the next sign, leaving behind the 21–29 degrees of the previous sign) in September 2015. Saturn's passage across these degrees and the precise turning point could—and was—calculated some years in advance. Some Astro-Forex traders were therefore unsurprised by this general downward trend.

They know too that Saturn will pass through the third decanate of Sagittarius (21–29 degrees) in 2017, and are already anticipating that once again the Euro will fall against the USD in particular.

Jupiter is said, in contrast to Saturn, to bring upward movement provided transits from the planet do not coincide with falls caused by Saturn. A good example is during the few weeks from mid-May 2013 to the Summer Solstice that year. Through these few weeks, Jupiter moved through the third decanate of Gemini (21–29 degrees). Unhindered by Saturn, Jupiter's passage through these degrees coincided with an increase in Euro value (against the USD).

Using this same technique, i.e. noting the movements of the Moon through the last decanate of any sign, is worthy of closer scrutiny. Note that the Moon changes sign roughly every two-and-a-half days: spending roughly two hours in each degree. There is a time span of around 20 hours every few days when a general change of trend should be noticeable as the Moon moves through the last 10 degrees of a sign. As yet insufficient research on this theory has been undertaken.

There is little doubt that lunar movement should be studied carefully, and that there are links between the lunar position and significant turning points.

Another method is to consider what happens as the Moon moves through the signs from Sagittarius to Aries—which it does every month. This transit, starting at Mercury's (trading planet) position in the Euro chart at 21 degrees Sagittarius, and then through an area of the horoscope covering risk and speculation, concludes as the Moon crosses the Descendant of the chart. Between June and October of every year, this will coincide with Full Moons in the signs Sagittarius, Capricorn, Aquarius, and

Pisces—though not on precise and correlating degrees with the Euro natal chart. This seasonal effect is most interesting—and potentially useful information to the astro-trader.

US DOLLAR

Unlike the Euro, there is no "start" date available for the US dollar. While the lack of a "start" date is unfortunate, there are charts and techniques that can be used to forecast likely trends. Many currencies fall into the category of "no launch date available." Astrologers then tend to look at the chart for the country itself while astro-traders employ another technique.

The astrologer's approach can be helpful. It is also of assistance to the astrologer if there is a recognized "Money related" Act (as with the United States and with the United Kingdom): thus yielding another date where the positions of the planets may be considered. In contrast, Astro-Forex traders consider the planetary formations at significant highs and lows (against another currency or, in the case of the US, the dollar index) and then explore the possibility of trading "reacting" to particular planetary conditions.

The generally acknowledged horoscope chart for the US dollar is based on noon (no recorded time available), April 2, 1792, Philadelphia, PA, when Congress passed the Coinage Act. The chart is given opposite. As there is no known time, no Ascendant or Midheaven is offered and the position of the Moon is given for midday, local time.

The US dollar has become the world's reserve currency. This is perhaps unsurprising given the strength of this chart where the Sun, in Aries, is trine to Uranus and also in applying conjunction to Saturn. If the Act was signed earlier in the morning, then the Moon could be exactly conjunct Uranus giving further strength to this chart. In any case, the conjunction of the Sun with Saturn and both in good aspect to the Moon/Uranus is indicative of a "me first" currency that commands—indeed, demands—respect.

We should note also the Grand Trine formation between the asteroid Ceres, the Jupiter/Neptune conjunction, and Pluto. The

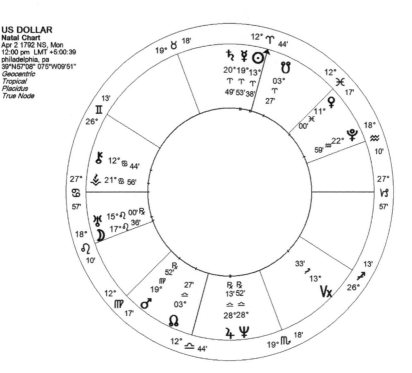

US DOLLAR
Natal Chart
Apr 2 1792 NS, Mon
12:00 pm LMT +5:00:39
philadelphia, pa
39°N57'08" 075°W09'51"
Geocentric
Tropical
Placidus
True Node

Jupiter-Neptune configuration in Libra speaks of the widespread use of the currency and the wishful thinking that it would be operated fairly.

Today we recognize that many US dollars are tainted—some quite literally—by drugs and money-laundering. These are the negative traits that may be seen through Venus' position in Pisces in trine to Chiron, and also of course by the Jupiter-Neptune conjunction. Yet this chart goes back to a time long before there was the widespread use of the narcotics in use today

Before using any chart for forecasting, it is important to "back-test" and see if events correlate with significant historical happenings. One obvious affirmation that this particular chart "works" is to test it against the date when President Nixon made his shock announcement to suspend the dollar's convertibility into gold in 1973. Even a cursory check shows there to be a link: Chiron, by transit, was moving over the Aries Sun position of this chart. It is important to note that Chiron had passed through the sign of Aries before, but what made the 1973 event stand out was that this transit coincided with Saturn in quintile (fifth of a circle aspect) to Uranus. This latter aspect speaks of both presidential authority and the shock of the announcement. A review of the earlier Chiron transits to the Sun reveals no other such coincidence. Students may enjoy working with this chart and back-testing against other significant events.

In forecasting the coming years using this chart, it must be noted that Pluto has not yet completed a full revolution and returned to its 1792 position—which it will do in the early 2030s. This could yet prove a revitalizing period for the US dollar: surely necessary after the buffeting it is likely to experience in the coming years.

In, 2019, Pluto will oppose the position held by Vesta in the April 1792 chart. Soon after this, Pluto challenges the Jupiter Neptune conjunction by forming a square aspect to it. Through 2019 and 2020, both Jupiter and Saturn reach conjunction with Pluto in Capricorn before going on to conjoin one another in the first degree of Aquarius. This is likely to be a highly volatile period for the world's banks, for the bond markets, and for foreign exchange generally. Together these transits may contribute to the dollar's displacement as the world's global reserve currency.

Transits, or comparisons of the position of the planets at any period to a single point in the past, are only part of the story. It is as important to consider transits to both Progressed and Directed positions. It is equally useful to use—as described at the end of the chapter on property—the Progressed Moon in declination chart (see opposite). To ease reading the graph, it looks at the twenty-year period from 2010, clearly showing a turning point in 2020 as the Progressed Moon reaches its maximum declination.

This shows a turning point mid-2020. Yes, this is part of the natural rhythm of this curve. The fact that this turning point coincides with the major transits listed above suggests that this particular turn will prove especially dramatic.

It is often the case that there is a crisis slightly ahead of these turning points. In this instance, Pluto's transiting opposition to Vesta in 2019 may be the key. Around this same time, Solar Arc

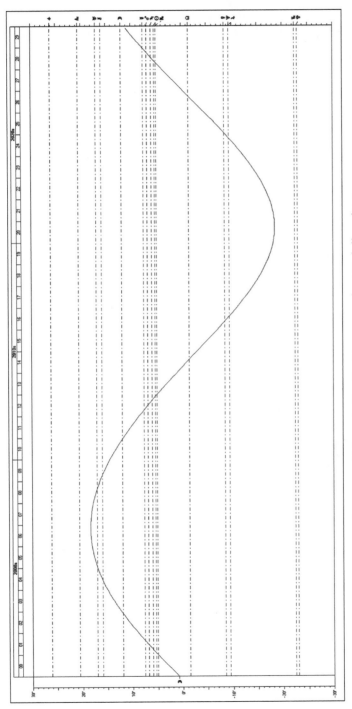

Progressed Moon in Declination curve for US dollar chart

Directed Pluto arrives at the nodal position for the first time in this chart's history. This may well be indicative of the undermining of the dollar strength following an intense power struggle.

It could be argued that US dollar's supremacy in the global marketplace has been compromised since the global financial crash. A former US comptroller has stated that US debt is close to $65 trillion (almost three times higher than the generally used figure) and that Americans may have "lost touch with reality" when it comes to spending. If he is correct, then the US could be brought to Earth with a Capricorn bump when Saturn aligns with Pluto in that sign at the end of the decade.

Within the first year of the quantitative easing announced after the 2008 crisis, Pluto, by transit, was at right angles to the nodal position of this dollar chart. The word "manipulation" is often used in connection with Pluto. It could be argued that quantatitive easing as Pluto squared the nodal axis was a manipulation of US debt—which at some point must surely be addressed. This could happen as Pluto edges toward the opposition to Vesta and the subsequent squares to both Jupiter and Neptune at the end of the decade. Certainly many factors point to the need to "re-balance the books" through these years. Before determining what this might mean, we should turn attention to the chart for the country.

There are long arguments as to the exact time that should be used for the USA national chart based on July 4, 1776. What is not in dispute is that the signing of the Declaration of Independence took place that day as the Sun was moving through Cancer. This is generally thought of as a "good" sign for family businesses. The Sun in a country's chart represent its leader. With the Sun in Cancer there is expectation that the leader will be "father of the country" and look after resources well. President Obama's financial mettle was surely tested within months of his inauguration which took place as Pluto, by transit, moved into Capricorn. Early on he discovered the "cupboard was bare." The USA, along with many other countries, was ill-prepared to cope with the global financial crisis.

In the July 1776 chart, Mercury (planet of commerce) is at 24

Cancer, with Pluto opposite at 27 Capricorn. Between 2020 and 2023, Pluto will oppose this Mercury. It is reasonable to deduce that this will be "crunch time" when re-evaluation of commercial activity is demanded. Though it could be argued that the dollar has been significantly—though not formally—devalued since the first tranche of quantitative easing, it has not yet suffered humiliation on the world stage. This scenario could yet occur at the start of the next decade. At the very least, commercial re-alignment is to be expected.

Given the links between the charts used for both the country and the US dollar, by virtue of planetary positions in both Cancer and Capricorn, and knowing that Pluto has yet to make major aspects to both toward the end of this decade and the opening of the next, it is possible to make a forecast with one chart that is confirmed by analysis of the other. That forecast—made through the astrologer's lens—must surely be that US dollar will lose value through 2019–23.

The Astro-Forex trader takes a different approach and considers the US dollar index over a period of years. Study then reveals which planetary aspects have coincided with major turning points. Between 2010 and 2015, the dominant theme was Uranus at apparent right angle to Pluto. From the geocentric perspective this took place on five occasions ending in March 2015. By the concluding aspect of the series, Uranus was at 15 Aries and Pluto at 15 Capricorn.

Perhaps it ought not to come as too much of a surprise to discover that whenever one of the faster-moving planets, Mercury, Venus, or Mars has come to 15–16 degrees of Aries, Cancer, Libra, or Capricorn, there has been marked reaction in this index. It may be that this response will now fade and that another zodiacal area assume greater voice: perhaps from the upcoming conjunction of Saturn and Pluto at 22 Capricorn. Certainly these degree areas warrant further attention.

The graph on the following page marks those dates in 2014 when the Cardinal degrees of 15–16 Cancer were crossed.

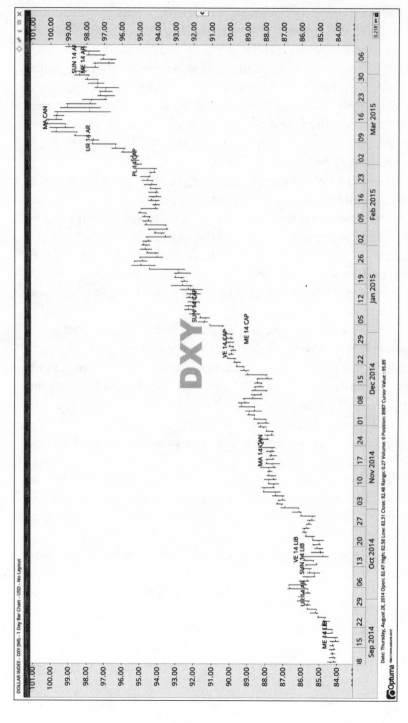

US DOLLAR INDEX with planets at 14 Cardinal

USD-CAD Relationship

Though both the USA and Canada celebrate their national days with the Sun in Cancer, the characteristics of the two nations are very different. So too are their currencies. Parity is rare and the astro-relationship of USD to CAD worthy of considerable research. Yet even cursory examination is revealing.

In November 2007, as Pluto passed the Galactic Center, one USD dollar bought just 0.9 CAD. A year later, after Pluto moved into Capricorn, it bought 1.3 CAD. The CAD, which was already losing against USD, fell further as Neptune moved into Pisces, gained as that planet retrograded back into Aquarius, and fell again when Neptune made its final (geocentric) Pisces ingress some months later. The point to make here is that a slow moving planet changing signs does appear to have marked effect. Slow-moving planets include Saturn, Uranus, Neptune, and Pluto. The planetoid Chiron must also be added to this list. It must be noted too that an ingress of any of these planets affects more than just one Forex relationship. It is not unusual for these planets to change signs within the course of a year but more common for there to be just one ingress in any twelve month period.

Chiron moves from Pisces to Aries in April 2018, and Uranus moves from Aries to Taurus that same year, while Saturn moves from Sagittarius to Capricorn: thus in the space of a few months, Saturn, Chiron, and Uranus all change signs. This may well result in a volatile period in foreign exchange markets. Neptune moves to Pisces in 2025 and Pluto to Aquarius in 2024: another twelve-month period that should see great change in this area of trading.

Using USD-CAD as an example: September 15, 2015 (Saturn's Sagittarius ingress) was a Friday. It was reasonable to expect that any pronounced movement between the two currencies would not take place until the following Monday—as indeed proved to be the case as shown below.

While an outer planet ingress demands attention, Forex traders benefit from the study of days of marked activity and reviewing any links between the faster-moving planetary cycles and significant turning points in currency trading.

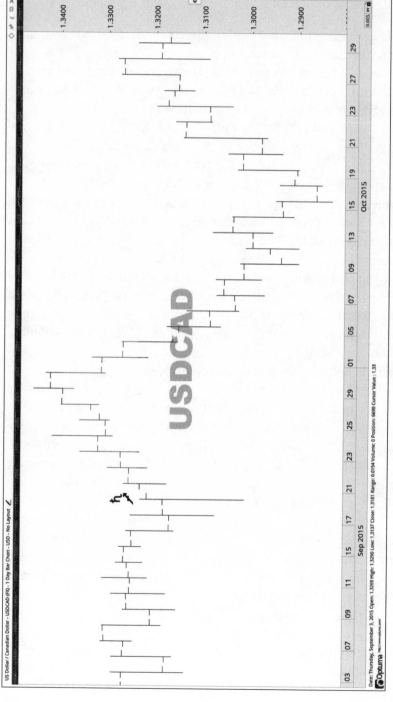

CAD to USD

In September 2012, the CAD bought 1.03 USD. On the day of that recent high, Pluto and Chiron were a sextile apart with Venus equidistant between the two. This planetary picture offers a possible clue to explore further. It does not take long to discover that Venus' position at the midpoint of Chiron-Pluto has been significant on other dates also. This planetary picture occurs roughly every six weeks and suggests a significant timing system to add to other trading methods. Determining the exact date and time of the aspect is not difficult, though assessing the direction and degree of adjustment in value between the two currencies requires considerable trading experience and the use of other (technical analysis) methods.

Both the USA and Canada with their Cancer Suns are ruled by the Moon. It is perhaps not so surprising that the relationship with their two currencies appears to respond to lunar rhythms. Aspects from the Moon to the Sun, planets, and asteroids occur and dissipate within a matter of hours: thus a trend grows and subsides. This is of a great importance to the Forex trader who can use this information to determine the exact time to buy or sell.

As with other proposed techniques, this study requires careful application. It is not simply a question of buying at one phase (e.g. New Moon) and selling at another (e.g. Full Moon). Though it might appear that a myriad of factors have to be taken into consideration, it is possible to focus on a few which, when used with technical analysis, assist in the determination of a trading strategy.

The number of factors to be examined can be contained. For example: in the case of the Moon-Mercury cycle—and as Mercury moves through all twelve signs in a year—it would be necessary to look at large periods of time to find comparisons (grouping together all those conjunctions in one sign). However, in the case of the Moon with a slow-moving planet, e.g. Pluto, for many years the conjunction of the Moon with Pluto would always be in the same sign (though not at the same degree). These conjunctions though apparently similar would differ in relation to the Sun-Moon cycle and also to the Moon's distance from Earth.

The impact of a Moon-Pluto conjunction where the Moon is at apogee or perigee would be expected to differ from one where the aspect takes place when the Moon is not in this extreme position.

BITCOINS

The Euro, USD, and CAD currencies have notes and coinage. One of the newer currencies to arrive in this new millennium has been Bitcoin: one of a group of new currencies, including Feather coin, China coin, etc. which have no physical characteristics. They are ideas: numbers on a page. These virtual currencies have no notes or coinage but are beginning to have major impact in global trading.

Bitcoin has already attracted significant attention from traders and investors. Though the actual time of first trade in this currency is unknown, the date for that event on January 3rd 2009 is a matter of public record. The creator of this currency is given as a Mr Satoshi Nakamoto who apparently first proposed the concept in 2008. Mr Nakamoto was assumed to be Japanese though perhaps not residing in that country. It may be that the name is a pseudonym and that the concept was the brainchild of a group of individuals.

Pluto had only recently entered Capricorn. It may be that the idea was being developed as Pluto crossed from Sagittarius into Capricorn. What is known is that first trade took place with Pluto in exact trine with Vesta. Aspects between Pluto and Vesta often coincide with major events in the currency markets e.g. the square aspect between the two coincided with devaluation of the Yuan in 2015.

The launch of Bitcoin was no doubt planned with precision. It may be that an astrologer was consulted. If not, then the date chosen may well have been a message from the Forex cosmos exchange—as the planetary signature on that day is highly significant.

Note that not only was there a stellium (Sun, Mars and Pluto) in Capricorn, but that there was unusual concentration of planets in the neighbouring sign of Aquarius as shown in its chart.

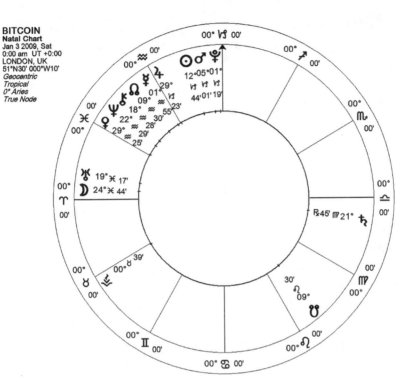

The chart shown uses the position of the planets at midnight, universal time, on the day of launch. It has not been possible to ascertain the time of first trade. The Moon moved from Pisces to Aries at 09.49 UT that day. Given that Bitcoin already stands out from the group of virtual currencies that have appeared in recent years, there are compelling reasons to think that the Moon had moved into Aries at the launch which may well have taken place after 09.49 UT. Aries is noted for pushing ahead, being out in front and generally initiating projects.

On its website, Bitcoin org gives this definition of its service:

Bitcoin uses peer-to-peer technology to operate with no central authority or banks; managing transactions and the issuing of bitcoins is carried out collectively by the network. Bitcoin is open-source; its design is public, nobody owns or controls Bitcoin and <u>everyone can take part</u>. Through many of its unique properties, Bitcoin allows exciting uses that could not be covered by any previous payment system.

(Astrologers will have no difficulty in identifying the mutual reception characteristics of Uranus and Neptune in this statement.)

While the position of the Moon may be open to conjecture, two things that cannot be disputed are that Pluto shared declination with the Lunar Node and that Mars, by declination, was out-of-bounds at extreme declination. The implications of these placements suggest a super-hero currency destined to go far and with the ambition to fight its way through to governmental (Capricorn) recognition.

Astrologers recognize that when Pluto's position is featured, then there is always the danger of manipulation, skull-duggery and generally unwelcome activity. Pluto is also sometimes described as the "tax collector." The underlying problem with this—and other crypto-currencies—is that they transcend borders, are effectively "anonymous" and that collection of tax and tracing transactions is, if not impossible, then at least very difficult. In years to come this could yet prove to be the "gangster's currency of choice."

Both Mercury and Pluto hold positions at 1 degree of, respectively, Capricorn and Aquarius, while Jupiter and Venus are at 29 degrees of those same signs. This is a most unusual picture that immediately draws the astrologer's attention: by transit, as a planet moves from one sign to another, it will first aspect both Jupiter and Venus (simultaneously) and then Pluto and Mercury. As we shall see, such transits have already coincided with strong trading trends.

Some have conjectured that Bitcoin is a shooting star, gaining attention now but destined to be forgotten before long. The chart for its first trade suggests something quite different.

As with the chart for the Euro, Pluto lies behind the Sun in the zodiac—so that in its early years, Pluto was approaching that Sun position. It has now successfully crossed this degree and is moving slowly toward Jupiter's position at the very end of

Capricorn: destined to reach this position in 2024. By this time Bitcoin is likely to be not just firmly established but could be a major player in currency trading.

The growing pains for this currency suggest it will be front page news between 2016 and 2019. Note how many examples of an 8–10 degree gap there are between planets in this chart. Using the solar arc technique, the implications of this are that through the years of Bitcoin's eighth to tenth anniversaries it will be challenged many times over. Given that this occurs post the major Pluto transit to its Sun, it seems likely that not only will it survive, but that it will assume increased importance on the world stage. That increased importance could be due to the less than wholesome activities with which it becomes associated.

An interesting point is that Bitcoin's Neptune is in exact conjunction with the USD's Pluto. It may yet be the case that Bitcoin insidiously undermines USD strength. Tempting as it may be to assume that activity on or near this degree would coincide with particular movements, this has not—at least as yet—been the case in XBT/USD trading history.

At Bitcoin's inception, Venus and Jupiter were each at 29 degrees of a sign and 30 degrees apart. It is very interesting to note that when these two planets opposed one another in November 2013, there was a major spike in Bitcoin's value. At this point, it reached $1212. As the aspect separated, Bitcoin's value fell, coming to a low point at the Jupiter-Pluto opposition in February 2014. The Venus-Jupiter cycle continues to be important however. The two planets formed a conjunction in August 2014— in Leo—which coincided with a marked (spiked) low in Bitcoin value ($248). The next Venus-Jupiter conjunction—this time in Virgo —Bitcoin was again on the rise. This though was part of a more complex configuration, as Mars too was moving through that sign. Bitcoin peaked at the Venus-Mars conjunction.

If Bitcoin's response to the Venus-Jupiter cycle continues, then it is entirely possible that a significant low will be reached when Venus and Jupiter form a conjunction at 29 Taurus on May 23, 2024. Venus and Jupiter form a conjunction every year of course but only in 2024 does the conjunction take place in the

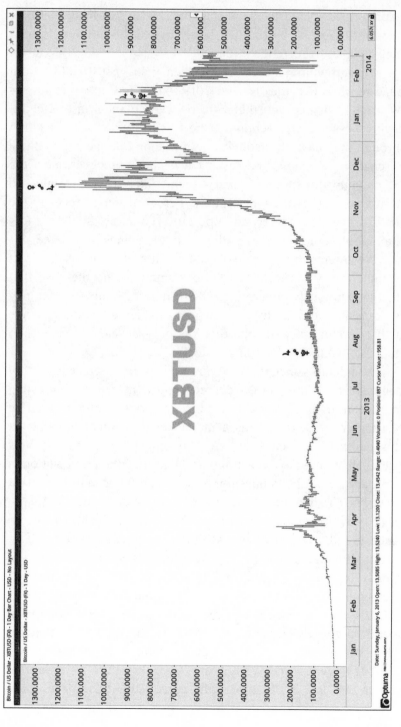

BITCOIN-USD

last degree of a sign—and so aspecting exactly the positions held in the natal chart.

For similar reasons we might wonder if a relative high will be reached on July 22, 2022, when Venus and Jupiter oppose one another. This opposition takes place across the Virgo-Pisces axis, actually at the start of those signs, but within tight orb of the natal positions.

CHAPTER SEVEN

COMMODITIES

This chapter considers the effect of planetary cycles on commodity prices: focusing on gold, silver, cotton, corn, oil, and sugar. As with currencies, actual "start dates" are rare. The lack of an initial horoscope is not a deterrent to those working in these areas however. Though the charts for key dates such as the first date of trading for silver on the Chicago Stock Exchange are used, forecasting more usually involves the study of transits and the planetary pictures these provide. As we shall see in this overview of probable trends, certain planetary positions have coincided with price turning points. If history does indeed repeat, then forecasts using these correlations should prove useful to traders and investors alike.

Both heliocentric and geocentric positions are important: whether studying indices, currencies, or commodities. In the case of the latter, heliocentric ingresses are important as we shall observe in this following brief overview of price movements in gold.

GOLD

Gold has been a valued commodity for millennia. A gold cycle of 55.8 years (three nodal cycles of 18.6 years) was identified by Y. T. Yong in 2004. He further posited an even longer cycle of three times this figure, 167.4 years which he linked to hyper-inflation and gold prices. His work examines links between this cycle and its half (a little over 83 years and closely linked to the cycle of Uranus around the Sun). Mr Yong's work is valuable in that the observable links between the nodal and Uranus' cycles suggest deviation in human behavior and endeavor which, in the financial world, are often related to movement in market prices.

For the purpose of forecasting the gold price over the next decade we will focus on recent price moves where data is available and verifiable.

Toward the end of the 18th century, the US Mint decided to peg the dollar to gold. In 1792 the price, per troy ounce, was set at $19.75. On only three occasions since then has the US government altered this value: in 1834 to $20.67, and a century later in 1934, to $35. The price was raised again in 1972 to $38, and in 1973 to $42.22. For the last four decades, the price of gold has been allowed to float freely: in 2011, reaching over $1880.

This relatively recent high price was no doubt a reaction to the global financial crisis. Some still feel that this price can yet be exceeded—despite the fact that the price has tumbled by $800 since that time. Many consider this market to be manipulated. Whether or not this is the case, the fact the remains that major moves in gold prices since 1972 can be shown to coincide with significant planetary formations. Correlation of distinct price points and resistance levels with certain planet ingresses, heliocentric planetary formations, and, from the geocentric perspective, the stations of Uranus, Neptune, and Pluto have been identified. Whether this provides sufficient information on which to establish a trading strategy is unclear. It would appear however, that used in combination with technical analysis, gains could be made.

A useful starting point is to consider a recent high and the planetary positions at that time. On July 1, 2011, the gold index was at $1440 (4 x 360: a significant number that would have been noted by W. D. Gann). The gold index (GLD) reached $1911 in late August before falling back a few dollars to $1884 on Monday 5th September 2011. The index then lost $200 in the space of just three short weeks.

One of the interesting things about that period is that Jupiter moved from Aries to Taurus. It entered that sign geocentrically in June and heliocentrically on September 1st. Taurus is associated with appreciation and wealth. We perhaps ought not to be surprised that there was a changed attitude—and subsequent increase in the price of gold through this period.

There was no strong link between the position of Uranus and the Lunar Node at this time but, in early September, Uranus made an aspect to the midpoint of Neptune and Vesta: arguably a contributory factor to a spike (Uranus) in price.

If Jupiter's transit of Taurus is relevant, we ought then to consider the price moves of approximately 11.88 years (Jupiter's orbit) earlier. We find that from the September Equinox to October 5, 1997, again slightly ahead of Jupiter's heliocentric Taurus ingress, the price moved from $255 to $339: a significant rise. The price then fell as Jupiter made its heliocentric Taurus ingress.

Using this simple detective work, we might reasonably expect a surge in the gold price in the weeks leading into Jupiter's next heliocentric Taurus ingress. Jupiter makes this Taurus ingress on July 10, 2023 after which date we should expect decline.

Of course, the next question is "decline from what"? and "Will there be a significant price rise before that date?." Perhaps we should bear in mind the conjunction of Uranus with the Lunar North Node in late July 2022. This might well mark a significant high and levels that are maintained for the better part of a year.

From the geocentric perspective, in September 2011, Jupiter was already moving through Taurus and had reached 10 degrees of that sign. Jupiter was also in exact parallel with Mercury in the early days of September that year. Moreover, in the days leading into September 5th, a trine had been building between the Sun and Jupiter while the asteroid Vesta was out of bounds at extreme declination. It is not unknown for the price of gold to rise a little in the days leading into Sun-Jupiter aspects as these dates are often chosen as celebratory dates (particularly for betrothals) in India especially. As it is customary to give gold to newly-weds, the price often lifts a little ahead of these dates.

During the course of every year, the Sun forms a conjunction with Jupiter, eventually moving through the various phases to reach opposition roughly six months later, before returning to conjunction. There are, roughly, 13 months between successive conjunctions.

As was pointed out above, astrologers in India see the dates on which the Sun and Jupiter form major aspects as bestowing blessings and so choose these dates for significant events (like weddings, as mentioned). In the main it would appear that they choose dates when the Sun and Jupiter are at the start of their cycle (conjunct), in sextile or trine (divisions of a circle by six or three). While it is possible to see minor upward shifts in price in the days ahead of these exact aspects, within this same cycle, other aspects provide information that could be more useful to the trader.

David Cochrane and his assistant Linda Berry have found distinct correlations between Sun-Jupiter septile aspects (multiples of a seventh of a circle) and gold price moves. Their study covered more than 40 years since the early 1970s. The results are compelling and should be added to the arsenal of trading tools deployed by those investing in this commodity.

One of the more interesting features of September 2011 and the high of $1880 is that this coincided with the asteroid, Vesta's, out-of-bound position. As explained earlier in the book, Vesta can be viewed as the trader's asteroid. It is often in prominent position when currency matters are in the news. Given the precarious state of many currencies after the global financial crash, it is perhaps not so surprising that as Vesta moved to an out-of-bound position, investors sought refuge in gold causing its price to rise. Note that the rise did not continue past the Sun-Jupiter aspect: turning instead and falling until the next major solar aspect: the Sun-Uranus opposition.

The graph on page 126 covers July–November 2011 with the aspects of the Sun to outer planets marked.

Gold recovered to $1794 by early November 2011. This was to prove a significant level. Though the price then fell, it returned close to this figure in February 2012 and again in October of that year. It is interesting to note that there were 90 days between the November and February dates and 270 between February and October. This number of days reflects the division of a circle by four. As W. D. Gann proposed, 45, 60, 90, 120, or 180, or 270 days, weeks, months, and years can be used as resonators. Seasoned traders will usually note at least 90 days from a significant high or low, with experienced traders marking these other time spans also.

On October 5, 2012 from the geocentric perspective, Saturn

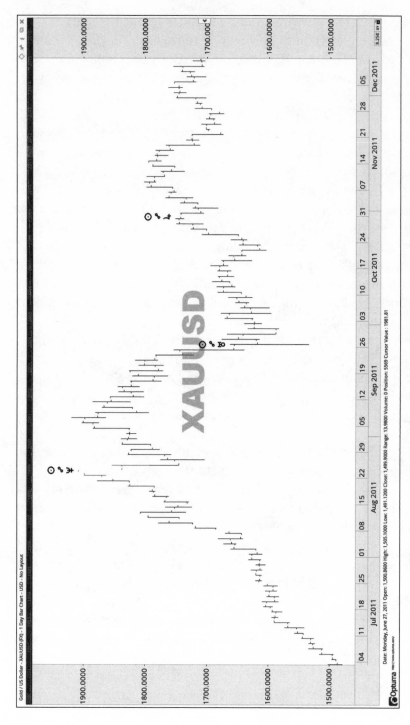

GOLD-USD July – November 2011 with Sun oppositions to Jupiter, Uranus and Neptune

moved into the sign of Scorpio (associated with mining). The Gold Index was $1790. From that date the price fell as Saturn made its way through Scorpio. At the time of writing it has yet to return to this level. When it does return to the $1790 apparent resistance line, it could then rise to figures well above this figure.

One possibility is that this return will be made in April 2020— 90 months following the October 2012 high. Another potential time frame would be 45 months later, in July 2016—when the price did indeed reach a high, though still some way off the $1790 figure. As will be seen below, a rather more likely period would be October 2017, 60 months from this date.

Gold "bears" are usually quick to point out that gold has few practical uses. Yet history shows it to be a valued commodity when other trust is gone. Given that we may well be headed toward a currency debacle at the end of the decade, it is entirely possible that gold will again find favor as currency issues escalate and that its price will rise accordingly.

If Saturn's presence in Scorpio was a factor in falling prices, Jupiter's arrival in that same sign from late 2017 could bring the opposite reaction. Prices may well rise and, given the position of other planets, escalate sharply.

The emphasis here must be on the word "could" as political factors may well come into play. There can be no certainty when only one planetary position is considered: a review of all the planets and the interplay of the various planetary cycles must be undertaken before a forecast is made.

Uranus is now moving through Aries and, heliocentrically, reaches the latter degrees of that sign in 2018. If this is indeed a sensitive area for gold price movements, then we should expect to see upward movement prior to Uranus' moves into Taurus on September 3, 2018. Yet Uranus transits often coincide with the unexpected.

To understand what might take place, it is a worthwhile exercise to consider the history of gold prices when Uranus last visited this area of the zodiac. Uranus moved through Taurus between 1934 and 1941. Students of economic history will know that the Gold Reserve Act was signed by President Roosevelt on

January 30, 1934. Section 2 of this act demanded the transfer of all monetary gold in the United States (including all coins and bullion owned and held by private individuals and institutions) to the US Treasury. These same owners received currency at a rate of $35 per ounce of gold.

The chart for this date is remarkable—not only because there was a lunar eclipse—but that the three planets Jupiter, Uranus and Pluto stood at apparent right-angles to one another at 23 degrees of three of the Cardinal signs. The "missing" sign is 23 Capricorn: within 1 degree orb of a Black Hole. A similar but not quite as exact planetary formation takes place in the early part of 2017 when once again Jupiter and Uranus oppose one another with Pluto—this time in Capricorn—between the two.

Another feature of the 1934 chart is that the sign of Aquarius was occupied by a group of planets: a planetary picture known as a stellium. An astrologer might interpret this as describing a highly political and, for some, ruthless decision. This planetary picture does not recur exactly in the coming decade but, as Uranus returns to its 1934 position, a similar alignment is worthy of attention.

In late December 2016, then three months later in March 2017 and again in September 2017, Jupiter and Uranus are once again be in opposition in similar areas of the zodiac to those of 1934. Pluto is again at right angles to the two planets but this time from the sign of Capricorn (in 1934, Pluto was moving through Capricorn's opposite sign of Cancer). True, Pluto is not at an exact right-angle as it was in 1934. However, through 2017, the apparent T-square is almost exact (geocentrically).

On certain dates, faster-moving planets and asteroids enhance this formation, e.g., in early March 2017, Vesta opposes Pluto effecting another and exact T-square involving Jupiter and Uranus while Pluto is close, but not quite exactly opposite. Over these same dates, Mars conjoins Uranus. True, this could indicate a currency (Vesta's involvement) or government bond debacle (Pluto in Capricorn). It could also have singular impact on the gold price. A possibility is that a government (not necessarily the US) will confiscate gold. Another is that there will be a collective, international decision to peg the gold price to a currency other than the US dollar.

Astro-traders are as interested in the influence of other, shorter cycles and correlation with gold price movement. Of these, the Mars-Jupiter cycle stands out—especially when dominant phases (conjunction, first and last quarter and opposition) accent the Mutable signs of Gemini, Virgo, Sagittarius or Pisces.

In 2015 for example, gold was expected to reach a minor high as Mars (geocentrically) conjoined Jupiter in Virgo on October 14th. The high was reached on October 15th with the price falling sharply in the succeeding days. Employing the strategy of marking 45, 90, and 120 days from this minor high, indicated key dates at the end of November 2015, mid-January 2016, and around February 11, 2016. The price did indeed fall, reaching a low on November 27th.

On January 18th, Mars and Jupiter were at 45 degrees of separation. This proved a significant turning point. From this date through February 11th the price rose from $1078 to $1261.

The influence as either planet moves through a Mutable sign is marked. Jupiter next reaches Sagittarius (Mutable) in November 2018. The first major aspect involving Mars in a mutable sign occurs on the 20th of that month with Mars in Pisces. This is the cycle's first quarter phase, the conjunction having occurred on January 7, 2018. This conjunction takes place in the "mining" sign of Scorpio and may well mark a high point. Though the price could fall immediately after this date, stronger downward movement is most likely after Mars moves from Mutable Sagittarius into Capricorn some weeks later—on March 17th.

Those trading gold frequently make use of lunar cycles. As we have seen with other examples, this is not as simple as monitoring the basic Sun-Moon cycle but takes into account seasonality. This provides research material with links between the conjunction of one cycle and the first quarter, then opposition and final last quarter of subsequent cycles. Welles Wilder studied this in great detail and discovered that short-medium and long term trends could be deduced. The reader will find this material well documented elsewhere.

PLATINUM

The price of platinum surged from 2005, peaking on March 3, 2008 at $2245. By late October 2008 the price had plummeted to $752. 2008 was, of course, the year of the global financial crisis when volatility was understandable. Even so, and accepting that planetary cycles do have an effect on prices, this surge ought to have coincided with significant planetary formations—as proves to be the case. Moreover, through understanding these, we may deduce that this price level will repeat.

In the days leading into the 2008 price peak, an exceptional planetary formation formed in the sign of Aquarius just as the Sun was moving toward conjunction with Uranus (one of the planets associated with that sign). Uranus moved through this sign between December 24, 2003 and 2010, forming annual conjunctions with the Sun during those years.

Aquarius is one of the Fixed signs of the zodiac and a link between this sign and items, services, and behavior that is unusual has long been recognized by astrologers. Earth metals can be considered to link with this sign with platinum near the top of the list. It is an unusual metal with a greyish-silver color that glints with an electric blue-purple under certain conditions: again reminiscent of the colors astrologers associate with Aquarius.

As we saw in an earlier chapter, the recent global financial crisis coincided with Saturn's opposition to Uranus: the two planets associated with the sign of Aquarius. Unusual activity in that sign might be expected to coincide with unusual activity in rare-metal markets.

In March 2008, Mercury, Chiron, Venus, Neptune, and the Node were all positioned in this sign: the first three in tight conjunction. This stellium is rare. Mercury and Venus pass through this sign annually, and the Node for approximately 18 months in as many years. Chiron will make this transit every half century and Neptune for a period of approximately a decade every 146 years. In fact, Chiron and Neptune have not shared this area of the zodiac in the last 500 years.

There will be no repeat of this planetary picture in the coming years: neither Uranus nor Neptune will return to this area of the zodiac in our lifetime. A conjunction of Saturn with Uranus (the ruling planets of Aquarius) will form in 2032—as Pluto transits that sign. Given that Pluto is sometimes described as the "God of Wealth," it is entirely possible that the price will soar then once more. However, there is not the same significant number of planets in Aquarius while the Saturn conjunction with Uranus is in operation.

A more likely period for a sharp upward movement in price occurs a decade earlier when Saturn forms a square to Uranus in 2021. Pluto will not have reached Aquarius by then but, in February of that year, there is remarkable emphasis on that sign when the Sun, Mercury, Venus, Jupiter, and Saturn form a stellium in Aquarius. Shortly we will compare the positions of the planets in February 2021 with those of March 2008. Links between the two could signal the return to this price level.

Before considering these periods, we should also consider the relationship between the high of March 2008 and the low in late October of that same year. Arguably the most important of these is that Chiron, in late October 2008, had retrograded to the exact position held by Mercury some six months earlier. As has been noted throughout this work, Chiron often brings reckoning and audit. In this instance we could consider that Chiron "told" Mercury to "stop with the pranks"—as it happens 240 days (another Gann measure) from the earlier high.

The dramatic downturn in price was exceptional and took place during the period of the global financial crisis—which perhaps goes some way toward explaining the severity of the move. Yet it does prompt the thought that planetary formations involving either the Fixed signs of Aquarius (the March configuration) or Scorpio (the October one) may be significant. In fact, analysis of turning points in the price of platinum shows that there is an above average likelihood of a price peak occurring when Fixed signs of the zodiac are involved.

Turning our attention to 2021, we find that in mid-February, Venus returns to the exact position held in March 2008, that the Sun will be on the degree held by the Node in 2008, and that both

Mercury and Jupiter hover over the degrees earlier occupied by Mercury and Chiron. Neptune will also be within a degree of the position held by Uranus. There is surely enough resonance and echo to suggest that February 2021 will see marked movements in platinum's price.

Of course this information is insufficient for the traders who, even if they accept that this month could mark a peak in prices, would surely wish to know when to buy in order to maximize profit. Given that escalation in the platinum price might well occur when Jupiter arrives in Aquarius, the investor might consider making purchase In the summer of 2020—perhaps when planetary attention is centered on Aquarius' opposite sign of Leo. Choosing a date, say 240 days before the expected high, could be considered if other technical indicators support this strategy.

SILVER

Silver has long been associated with the Moon: so it should come as no surprise that the price of this special metal tends to move with lunar rhythms. As we know, the Moon moves through all 12 signs of the zodiac during the course of a month: the very definition of the period. It does not however keep a regular distance from the Earth; the variation in distance results in the Moon moving quickly through some signs and slower through others. As might be expected, when there is a fast Moon, the price of silver tends to move more quickly than during those times when the Moon is slow.

Turning points in the price of silver often correlated with New or Full Moons or with the Moon reaching maximum North or South declination, or when the Moon is at apogee or perigee, or at maximum or minimum latitude. These four rhythms are of considerable import: when the cycles coincide—as when the Moon is Full, at maximum declination, and/or at apogee or perigee—the reaction of traders tends to be volatile, and so pushing prices up or down. True, this affects all markets. In the case of silver however, the effect can be dramatic.

In 2009, the strategy of buying silver a week ahead of the apogee and selling on that date, would have produced a profit on 12 of 13 occasions. This strategy was less successful in 2010 as Uranus and Neptune moved into mutual reception—though taken together with technical analysis still provided useful clues to positive trading opportunities.

The Moon reached maximum possible declination in 2005–06 and again in 2015. Between the June Solstice in 2005 and the May Full Moon of the following year—and through the period of lunar maximum declination—the silver index rose from $7 to $15. The price fell after that Full Moon to a low of $9 by the June Solstice of 2006. An in-depth study of this period will be offered in a later work.

The graph on the next page shows the rise in price through 2005–06.

Silver traders of the last twenty years have lived through exceptional conditions. They have witnessed price moves that did not occur in earlier years suggesting a review of the position of the outer (slow-moving) planets through this period. One fact stands out: Uranus and Neptune have each moved into Aquarius in the last twenty years. Note that some generations never live through Neptune's transit of this sign. Uranus' eighty-four year orbit of the Sun is also relatively lengthy and some traders would not have been in employment and trading this metal as Uranus last moved through this area of the zodiac.

Both Jupiter and Saturn have also transited this sign in the last twenty years. When Jupiter made its Aquarius ingress in January 2008 the price was a little over $11. By the time Jupiter moved into Pisces a year later, the price was $33. A return of this size would be of considerable interest to an investor.

Saturn might be expected to depress prices; yet this was not the case during Saturn's most recent transit of this sign. Saturn last moved through Aquarius in 1991 and made its final passage into Pisces in 1994 (having retrograded between the two signs). During Saturn's transit of Aquarius, the price moved from $3.8 to $5.3. Again, a rise of 50% over a two-and-a-half year period would be of interest to an investor.

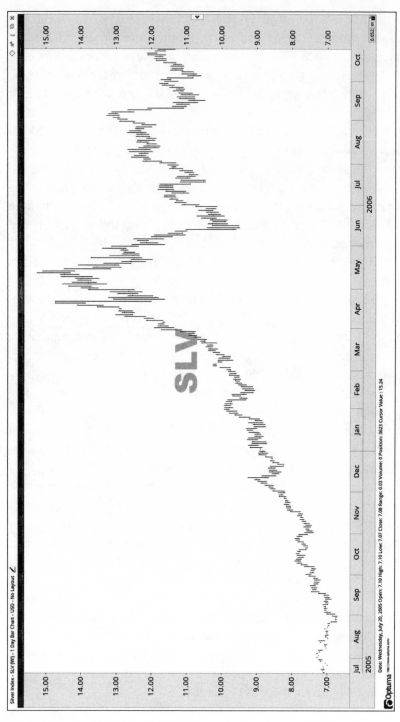

SILVER INDEX JULY 2005–2006

This information is particularly important as both Jupiter and Saturn will be moving through that sign from their conjunction in December 2020. These two planets have not conjoined in this sign since the conjunction sequence in Air signs: in 1226, 1285, 1345, and 1405.

From December 2020 through until December 2021, moves in silver prices could be dramatic. This mirrors the probable price moves in platinum within this same time frame. The stellium of planets in Aquarius in February 2021 may see silver prices surge in a similar way to those of platinum. Both have particular practical use in developing technologies that could act as a spur to price rises as demand increases.

Unusually, there is a useful horoscope for silver. This uses the first trading of the commodity on the Chicago Exchange in July 1933. (See chart below.)

There are several very interesting features of this chart. Firstly Chiron is at a right angle to the nodal axis and Ascendant,

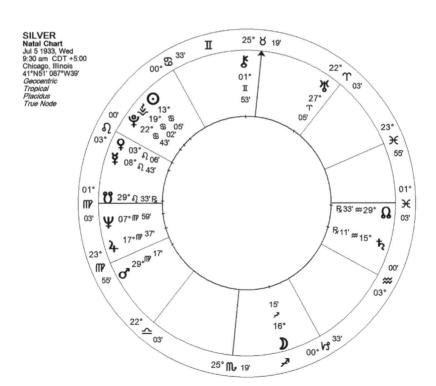

SILVER
Natal Chart
Jul 5 1933, Wed
9:30 am CDT +5:00
Chicago, Illinois
41°N51' 087°W39'
Geocentric
Tropical
Placidus
True Node

and secondly Saturn is half-way through the sign of Aquarius and therefore at the midpoint between Solstice and Equinox. Note too that the Lunar Node (always moving backwards through the signs) had recently moved from Pisces to Aquarius.

The Moon's passage through the sign of Sagittarius each month also appears to have particular effect: often lifting the price during the hours in which it transits this sign, and especially so if lunar apogee coincides (as in 2009).

It is Saturn's position at 15 Aquarius that may be the most important factor of all however. The very fine financial astrologer Jack Gillen, noted that the position of the Moon in the chart for the Sun's return to this degree provided useful information for that year's silver trading. In this, the position of the Moon by sign and aspect is given attention.

OIL

Astrologers associate Crude Oil with the planet Pluto and refined oil with Neptune. At the time of writing, oil prices have fallen substantially. Whereas at one time crude oil reached a high of over $140, it has fallen to less than $40 since the global financial crisis. There is now increasing concern as to when this level will rise as at these low levels, for some, the cost of extraction is greater than the price.

It is certainly true that there has been a considerable decline in price since Neptune entered Pisces; with some of the opinion that the price will not rise substantially until Neptune leaves that sign in 2025. It is not yet even at the half-way point of its transit of this sign. Coinciding with Saturn's squares to Neptune through 2016, prices have been, at times, $100 less than their all-time high. Saturn joins Neptune in Pisces between 2023 and 2026, during which period oil could reach presently unthinkable lows.

This is not to say that oil prices will be in steady decline in the coming decade. If attention is given to solar cycles, demand for oil (and energy of all kinds) is likely to increase through 2018 to 2020 if a solar minimum occurs on cue. Indeed, the approaching minimum may be of longer duration than average. Recall that several planets will be grouped at one side of the Sun (Jupiter, Saturn, and Pluto) and that during December of 2019 and January 2020, Mercury and Venus will join them. This suggests a singular pull on the Sun which could have a dramatic effect on its "normal" rhythms. Through this period , the Moon will at its closest to the Earth: another phenomenon indicating disturbance to weather patterns.

Demand for energy: whether for air-conditioning, transport fuel, or for heat is likely to be great and with that, increased demand for oil. Its price may well rise, allowing those who "own" the oil to raise prices.

The cycles of Mars with Neptune, and Mars with Pluto also yield valuable information for the oil trader who may be particular interested in the conjunctions made by Mars and Neptune since Neptune's Pisces ingress in November 2011. The square aspect between these two planets (taken either geo or heliocentrically) has coincided with very definite turning points at which prices have commenced a downturn. Between 2011 and 2015 Mars completed two orbits of the Sun. Each square or opposition with Neptune coincided with a minor rise followed by a downturn in oil prices.

This was also true of the conjunction in February 2013 but not true of the one in January 2015. The latter warrants close inspection. Saturn had recently entered another of the Mutable signs. This conjunction marked a low from which the price rose (not consistently) through to the square. Mars made its square to Saturn not long before its conjunction to Neptune. It may be that the former aspect "arrested" the price decline. As Saturn moves faster than Neptune this pattern will not repeat in the near future. It is more likely that the annual conjunctions of Mars with Neptune between 2016 and 2025 will coincide with minor highs, and that for at least a six-week period (mirroring earlier declines), oil prices will tumble.

The much shorter cycle of Sun and Pluto also has resonance for oil prices. In particular, the trine or 120 degree aspect has marked tops. A possible strategy would be to buy at the conjunction or opposition prior to this aspect. In the case of conjunction to trine, the period would be about twice that of opposition to trine.

Though oil has been around for millennia, there is a chart for the moment the first barrel of crude was captured in Titusville, Pennsylvania. This chart neatly reflects the importance of oil through the last century-and-a-half. Neptune's position in this chart is at 26 Pisces. Neptune makes a return to this position in 2024, perhaps marking the moment when oil ceases to have the political importance it has held throughout this last orbit.

CORN

Those trading this commodity using planetary cycles focus their energies on short cycles: the Moon-Mercury cycle in particular capturing their attention.

It is not a case of buying at the conjunction and selling at the opposition, as the actual time at which aspects take place is important. Those trading corn using the Chicago Exchange, take note of the times when this Exchange is open for business: Those trading hours are 9:05am to 1:00pm local time Chicago. (There is also the open outcry; 6:30pm to 6:00am electronic exchange). It would be rare (for example) for a Moon-Mercury opposition to take place at the exact moment that the exchange closes for the day—though highly relevant should that be the case

The following graph shows corn price movement in 2015. The corn price mid-June was $350. On July 16th it touched $438. Clearly those who bought in June and sold in July did well. The big question is whether those July dates could have been selected.

The astro-trader would first note Jupiter's Virgo ingress on August 11th (geocentric). Heliocentrically this ingress would take place on July 14th. The latter perspective would capture this trader's attention. An almost reflex reaction would be to see what happened 11.88 years ago (a Jupiter cycle) when similar conditions occurred. On September 5, 2003, Corn made a high

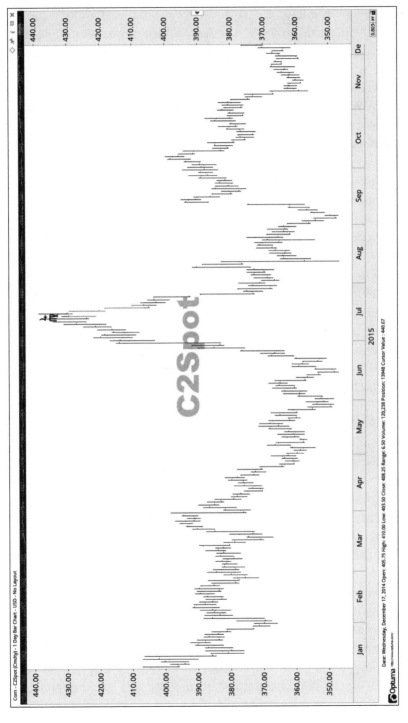

CORN 2015 WITH JUPITER'S HELIOCENTRIC SIGN CHANGE

of $244 from a low of $211 a few weeks earlier. During a Jupiter cycle before that in 1991, the heliocentric ingress took place in late October and also marked a top before prices then declined. Even with this cursory overview it is reasonable to expect that corn will reach a high twelve years from now on May 23, 2027.

The geocentric perspective is no less important. Once again the price rose (to $388) from a low of $370 just a week earlier. Of considerable interest is what took place on the day of the actual ingress when the price ranged between $376 and $388. Catching the optimum moment to trade that day required particular attention to detail: specifically to the aspects made by the Moon and Mercury. These two had formed a conjunction mid-June and reached their next conjunction on July 15th (coincident with Jupiter's heliocentric ingress). It is essential for the astro-trader to be familiar with both geo and heliocentric perspectives. When events in both systems coincide, strong market reaction is likely.

Determining the actual price levels is for another book. Suffice it to say here that the major price move between the $211 low and the $244 level is a difference of $33—the exact number of degrees traveled by Mercury (geocentrically) between the low and high.

Each of these dates is then studied with particular attention given to Moon-Mercury aspects. One date stands out: Thursday September 3rd when, as the Chicago Exchange opens, the Moon opposes Mercury exactly. That same day a T-square formation, with Mars square the position of Venus and Saturn confirms this as a day when market reaction is likely to be strong. The Moon-Mercury opposition is itself at a right angle to the Galactic Center: further underlining the probability of market volatility.

This overall planetary picture immediately suggests a turning point—and a probable low. Of course, the trader wants to know from when and by how much? One possibility would be to suggest a downturn from the conjunction (August 19th) preceding this Moon-Mercury opposition. Given that the expected move should be particularly marked, it seems reasonable to anticipate that any movement will be of long duration—covering weeks rather than days. Should there be a down-turn, then this could begin mid-

July when the Sun (in Cancer) opposed Jupiter, Saturn and Pluto within a matter of days.

Added to technical analysis undertaken in 2020, it ought to be possible to come up with a useful strategy taking full advantage of the astro-knowledge we have for that early September 2020.

SUGAR

There is little doubt that price movements in certain soft commodities correlate with the movement of planets through particular areas of the zodiac.

Sugar prices reached an all-time high of $65.20 in November 1974 as Uranus entered Scorpio (geocentric) having risen from a low of $1.25 in January 1967 as Jupiter (again geocentrically) arrived in Cancer. Though the dates of these ingresses do not match exactly with the realized turning point, the closeness of the event is sufficient for us to alert the sugar-trader to be aware of the potential for similar events in the month when an outer planet changes sign.

From the astrological perspective sugar is associated with the planet Venus which rules the signs of Taurus and Libra. It might be anticipated that the transit of unpredictable Uranus through either of these signs would coincide with unusual price moves. As Uranus moved through Libra (1968 to 1974) the sugar price did indeed rise—and to unprecedented levels. Uranus will reach this sign again in 2051: at which point prices may well soar until they reach a peak as Uranus arrives in Scorpio in 2058.

Perhaps unsurprisingly, the Venus-Mars cycle has proved useful in forecasting turning points in this market. The conjunction and first square of this cycle has had particular effect in recent years.

COTTON

The legendary W. D. Gann noted that when the two planets Uranus and Neptune formed aspects during the sowing periods of any year, there was greater likelihood of flooding of the Mississippi river and, therefore, high probability of those crops being damaged. This would result in shortage and prices would likely soar as a result. This valuable research enables us to determine with some precision which years in the future are likely to be problematic as regards flooding in this region. The two form a contra-parallel aspect in February 2017 suggesting a problematic year. Rather more serious are the sextiles of 2027 and the quintile aspects of 2033. What may yet go down as the worst flooding for over half a century could coincide with the square aspect between the two planets in 2040.

CHAPTER EIGHT

TIME AND PRICE

PART ONE

Our exploration of the financial universe must include the link between time and price. The conversion of planet longitude to price was a key method used by W. D. Gann. In recent years his commendable research has been followed by the works of Daniel Ferrera and Olga Morales. This chapter offers a brief review of a system, not dissimilar to theirs, that can be put to immediate use: the conversion of planetary longitude to price to determine probable resistance levels in any index or equity.

Using a modern ephemeris, we can look up exactly where a planet will be (or where it was) at any time in the future or past. The trader is interested in using such positions to predict actual prices. Once the value of an index or stock starts to rise, the trader welcomes a forecast not just of when the price might peak or bottom, but also at what level. Considerable work has been done in this area and this chapter can only give a brief overview of the techniques used.

A commonly used system is to convert each degree of longitude to $1. This is not the only scale in use: there are times when it is more appropriate to use 50¢ per degree, or $10. There are no hard and fast rules. Daniel Ferrera's system is intriguing and offers a complex scaling model worthy of research.

For the moment we will focus on $1 per zodiac degree: For example, Pluto is presently passing through the sign of Capricorn and on January 1, 2017 will have a position of 287 degrees of longitude. We can interpret this longitude value as a price of 288, or, for lower prices (where the scale used is 10¢ or even 1¢), 2.88 or 28.8. This precise figure will have resonance for some stocks which are likely to meet resistance levels of, e.g. $288, $2.88.

In the case of indices operating in the thousands, multiples of 360 must be added to yield other "Pluto Lines." For example, the Dow Jones index is in the many thousands. To find Pluto's line in relation to this index, we need to count through multiples of 360

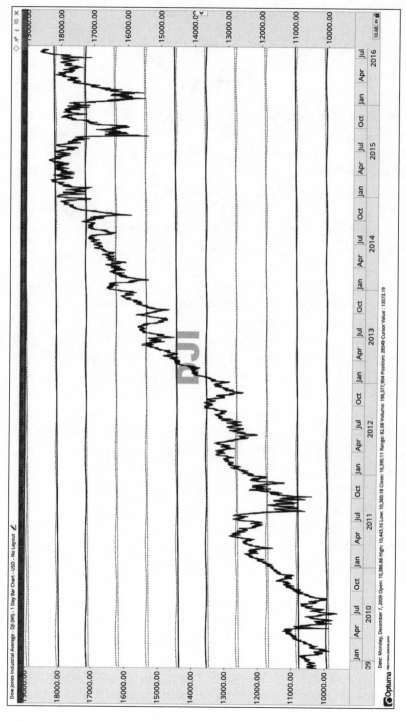

Dow Jones Index with Uranus and Pluto lines covering 90 degree relationship (cycles of the zodiac) before arriving at a figure that is less than 360. At 16,000, the Dow Jones Index would be 44 x 360 (15840) plus 160 points. At 16,128, that index would be resonating on the Pluto line. (1628 is 44 x 360 + 288: the Pluto position in our example).

There are subsidiary Pluto lines. These occur at 90, 180, and 270 degrees from the base position. Some people also take into account subsidiary lines at multiples of 45 degrees while others (particularly day-traders) use multiples of 15 degrees from Pluto's position. The latter system makes for rewarding study: as when Pluto is in aspect of a multiple of 15 degrees from another planet, the two planet lines coincide, often marking a level of considerable interest.

Share prices do not reach the levels of indices where, for example, 44 times 360 must be considered. Values are considerably lower. Amongst these numbers would be 1008 (720 + 288), 1368 (1080 + 288), 1728 (1440 or 4 x 360 plus 288) and 2088 (1880 + 288). Subsidiary Pluto lines can also be calculated: the most usual set of subsidiaries being units of 90 from the converted planet position (in this instance 288 plus 90 = 378, and 288 + 180 = 468, or 288 + 270 = 558).

You will recall that between 2010 and 2015, the two planets Uranus and Pluto were often at right angle to one another. This aspect was the first hard aspect between the two planets since the 1930s. Astro-traders were confident that reverberations would be felt through global stock markets and that the planet lines linked to the degrees involved would mark clear resistance levels. The graph below covers the Dow Jones Index through these years. It is tantalizing that so often the combined Uranus and Pluto and their subsidiary lines (plus 90, 180, etc) provided expected levels.

The task of preparing a planetary line graph should be carried out twice: once using heliocentric motion and then again using geocentric motion. This is particularly important when preparing planet lines for Mercury, Venus, and Mars. The next two graphs show Mercury lines for 2015 first using the heliocentric positions and then the same period shown geocentrically.

As outlined in an earlier chapter, Jupiter and Saturn, Jupiter

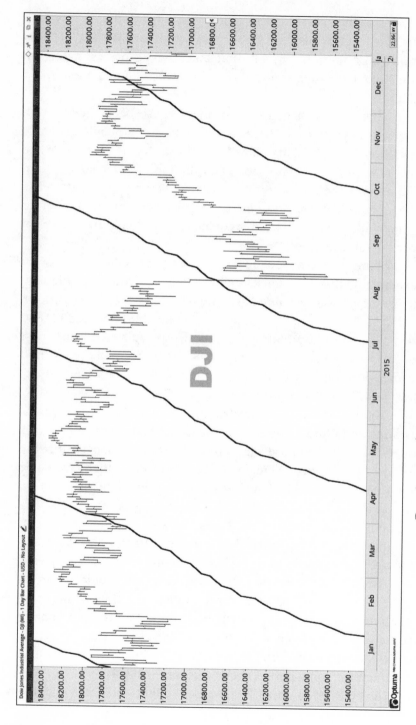

Dow Jones Index with Mercury heliocentric lines 2015

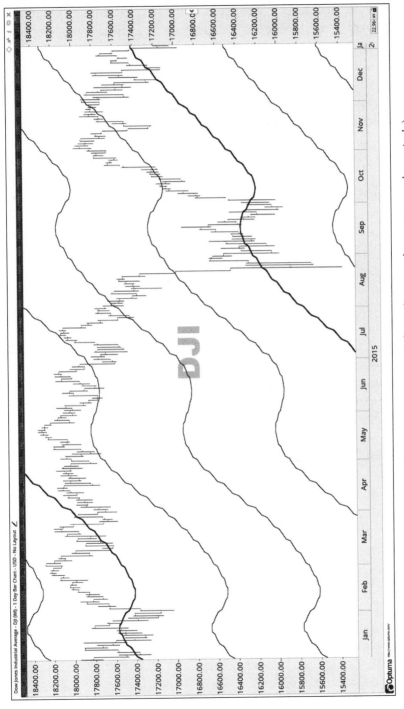

Dow Jones Index with Mercury geocentric lines (curves show retrograde periods)

and Pluto and Saturn, and Pluto each form conjunctions between 2019 and 2020. The actual degrees at which each of these alignments occur suggest the resistance levels for that period. As both heliocentric and geocentric positions must be considered, this will result in two sets of figures. Both have relevance. When this information is combined with good technical analysis, the experienced astro-trader will know which to use and when.

The Jupiter-Saturn conjunction is particularly important. We know this to be the first such conjunction to form in Aquarius since the 13th century. The energy or vibration this brings will likely be experienced across all markets. The start of Aquarius relates to the figure 300. For all indices then there will be Jupiter-Saturn resistance at multiples of 360 plus 300. To this we could also add squares (90 degree units).

Prior to this significant conjunction Saturn and Pluto align in Capricorn on January 12, 2020 at 22 Capricorn. With Saturn then moving through an area of the zodiac with which it has particular affinity (Saturn is said to rule Capricorn), this conjunction is likely to be felt strongly across all markets. This degree area translates to multiples of 360 plus 292. Assuming that the Dow Jones Index has not fallen below 10,000 by this time, possible resistance levels would include 11092 (30 x 360 + 292), 11452, 11812, 12172, 12532, etc.

As the above listed planets move relatively slowly, these figures are of interest but not always useful to the trader working these markets daily or weekly. It is more common for astro-traders to use the planetary lines of faster moving planets. Whereas with the Uranus-Pluto example given above the lines appear almost straight, in the case of any of the inner planets (Mercury, Venus and Mars), their respective planet lines appear bent: reflecting their retrograde periods.

The graph opposite is used to illustrate the effect of geocentric Venus lines on the Dow Jones Index in 2015. Note the very large down turn in this index during Venus' retrograde period and how the top and bottom levels were marked by Venus lines. Though it is usual to use the subsidiary lines that mark 90, 180, and 270 degrees as well as the actual planet line other aspects are

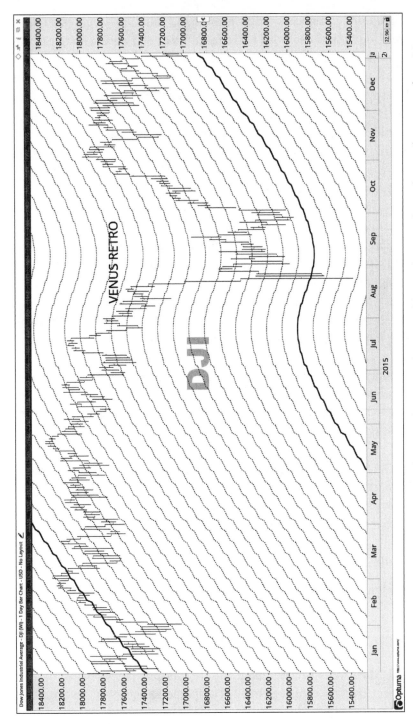

Dow Jones Index with Venus geocentric lines and retrograde. Dotted lines show each 15 degree from actual position considered: including multiples of 45 and 60 degrees. Those working with these lines find that units of 15 degrees (a twentieth of a circle) are most useful.

In this example, and to illustrate the level of detail that can be applied, these units of 15 degrees are given. Even smaller units are explored and used by some astro-traders. Where lines formed by, for example, Venus coincide with lines formed by, for example Uranus (as the two planets form an exact aspect to one another), astro-traders often find that the level reached bears a direct relation to an important price point.

This can also be seen when the Mars-Uranus "crash cycle" is scrutinized. It has been observed that markets tend to rise in the period between the sextile (when the two are 60 degrees apart) and their opposition. This latter phase of their cycle often marks a significant top. Heliocentric and geocentric graphs showing these aspects are given in the graphs on pages 151 and 152). In the heliocentric version shown opposite, note that the top was reached a few days beyond what might have been expected. The expected downward movement occurred but was triggered by another event related to geocentric aspect activity. This does not invalidate the importance of the heliocentric perspective which offers a marker for timing but needs to be used in conjunction with geocentric positions and aspects.

The geocentric Mars-Uranus opposition of December 2013 coincided with the December Solstice. The astro-trader considered that this would bring a significant high in the DJI. The accompanying graph is of the DJI with the Mars planet line marked (in green). Our trader then anticipated that the high reached at the Mars-Uranus square some months earlier would likely be breached. From the level reached at that high, this trader, using increments of 15 from Mars' transiting position, could judge with reasonable accuracy the probable levels that the DJI might reach. This information, together with sound technical analysis confirmed the value of having planetary lines as part of their trading tool-box.

Mars was retrograde through this period resulting in this aspect occurring three times within the space of a few months.

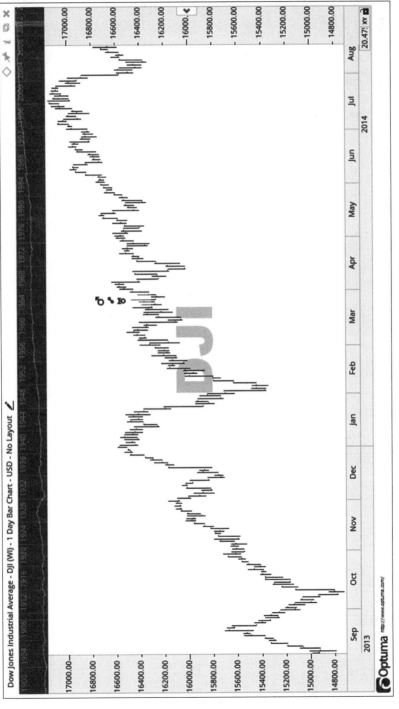

Mars–Uranus heliocentric opposition

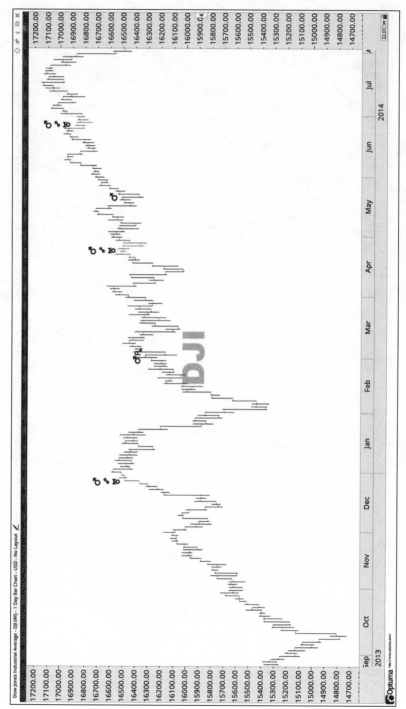

Dow Jones Index showing Mars and Uranus geocentric oppositions, retrograde and Mars' line

The astro-trader singled out the opposition coinciding with the Solstice as being the most significant of the three, but kept a watchful eye on these lines, anticipating that the index could touch this level on the other two occasions. As should be clear, the astro-trader keeps an eye on the positions of all planets and the Sun: noting especially those dates when geometric patterns are exact. The Sun's passage over either Solstice (approximately June 21st and December 21st of each year) and either Equinox (approximately March 21st and September 21st) is also deemed to have extra import.

TIME AND PRICE

PART TWO

Using the timed data of an IPO, a slightly different technique can be employed. This technique compares time and price with the Sun and planet positions on a particular day and at a specific time. The following examples show how this technique can be used. Those who have mastered predictive astrological techniques (progressions and directions) should find this technique easy to implement.

Example 1

GOOGLE

Google's Initial Public Offering (IPO) was on August 19, 2004 at 09.30 EDT and would not have been the only stock on offer that day. Deciding to invest in this stock required the astro-trader to study both the company prospectus and the chart for that moment. It is never wise to invest solely on the basis that the chart for an IPO appears "good"! If an investor chooses to add astrological analysis to decision making, then there are many factors to take into account: the planetary formations on that date and, peculiar to that exact time in New York or place of IPO, the position of the Ascendant, Midheaven and Vertex.

The Sun passes through all 360 degrees of the zodiac each year. Of these degrees some are especially important: the Summer and Winter Solstices (approximately June 21 and December 21) and March and September Equinoxes (approximately March 21 and September 21). The half way points between these dates also carry particular emphasis (roughly February 4th, May 5th, August 4th, and November 4th). Generally, stocks launched on these dates have high momentum surging or failing quickly. Another date to be considered as having extra power is August 19th when the Sun aligns with the "Royal" star, Regulus.

There are, of course, a myriad of Fixed Stars. Some are deemed more important financially than others however and alignment with these seems to bestow certain characteristics to the relevant dates. Astro-traders take note of companies whose IPO's occur around the date when the Sun is conjunct certain Fixed Star positions they consider to bring extra influence.

Noting the alignment of the Sun with Fixed Star, Regulus, at this IPO date, this trader might reasonably have predicted great things for stocks brought to market that day. In Google's case, the initial price was indeed exceeded within hours. So successful has this stock been that in Google's first 10 years of trading, those who purchased at initial IO saw a return of 1293%.

(A key date in Google's history was April 12, 2012 when a two-for-one split was announced. Google shares, which were then trading at around $650, saw an initial a dip to half that amount: roughly $325 per share as we would expect with the split though the price subsequently rose to over $700).

To return to the IPO chart: the astro-trader notes the distribution of planets through the signs of the zodiac. Here there is clear emphasis on the sign Virgo—with three planets in that sign. Accent on planets in Virgo immediately suggests focus on practicalities and a 24/7 willingness to work. The astro-trader would also be excited by the position of the Moon so close to the Ascendant. The Moon says much about the public's reaction to a stock. Within just a few degrees of the Ascendant, this suggests great public interest. True, this also indicates an interest likely to wax and wane suggesting high volatility. Even so, this trader

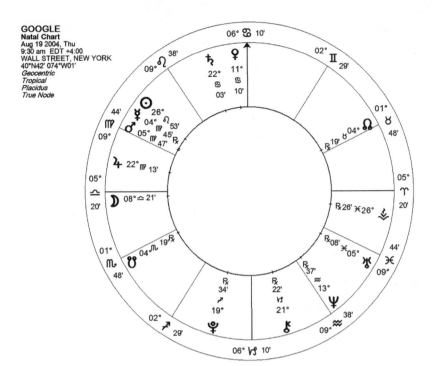

GOOGLE
Natal Chart
Aug 19 2004, Thu
9:30 am EDT +4:00
WALL STREET, NEW YORK
40°N42' 074°W01'
Geocentric
Tropical
Placidus
True Node

would anticipate this being a potentially exciting stock worthy of his or her investment.

Attention would also have been drawn to the position of Venus very close to the Midheaven amplifying the probability that this would be a popular—perhaps even a "much loved" stock. In time, Google might also be referred to as a "beautiful stock" to own.

Note that Venus is not placed EXACTLY on the Midheaven but is positioned exactly 5 degrees from it. This apparent "gap" between the two puts the experienced astro-trader on alert. Using one particular forecasting system, it indicates the potential for this stock to soar in value at around age five (in 2009). That same forecasting system would be used to note that the Sun, at 26 Leo would progress to Virgo a little over three years from the IPO, in 2007—and coinciding with the Ascendant progressing to the lunar position where there is again a difference of around 5 degrees.

History records that three years after the IPO, and as the Progressed or Directed Sun moved from Leo to Virgo, in May 2007, Google implemented Universal Search. The share price rose from $231 to $275, a rise of 19% in the space of two months.

Two years later, in December 2009, five years after the IPO, and as Solar Arc Directed Venus moved to conjoin the Midheaven at launch, Google offered real time search results: once again lifting the share price.

Note there that two different systems have been deployed: the system of Secondary progressions and Solar Arc Directed progressions. An explanation of these methods is given at the end of this chapter (see page 172).

This rough and ready system of marking the difference in number of degrees between Ascendant, Midheaven or their opposites (Descendant and IC), and a planet position requires no complex mathematics and gives a useful guide as to which years are likely to be key for the stock involved. The two-for-one share split nine years after the initial IPO came at exactly the number of degrees between the Sun and Mars, ie. in the year when the Sun progressed through 9 degrees to conjunction with Mars.

The table below shows the positions of the planets and key astronomical points (including Lunar Node) for the IPO for Google. Just as we learned that the position of a transiting planet could be converted into a price point for the Dow Jones Index, we can convert the positions of the planets at an IPO to price. The astro-trader would anticipate these price points featuring in Google's stock price movements. The first task is to list important points from the IPO chart and, assuming $1 per degree, list these in order from the lowest figure (the lowest figures covering positions in Aries and the highest those positions in Pisces). The result is as follows:

$14	Vertex
$35	North Node
$96	Midheaven
$101	Venus
$112	Saturn

$146	Sun
$154	Mercury
$155	Mars
$172	Jupiter
$185	Ascendant
$188	Moon
$215	South Node (North Node + 180 degrees)
$226	Part of Fortune
$259	Pluto
$291	Chiron
$313	Neptune
$335	Uranus
$356	Vesta

These are of course the INITIAL or "natal" positions. Though they retain their importance for the lifetime of a company's trading, the progressed positions must also be calculated and converted to price.

Google's Trading Story

Google had originally intended to set the opening price at over $100. This was then changed to $95 and the final offering made at $85. A choice has to be made as to which price-degree ratio to use. The astro-trader must first consider how best to convert this price to degrees: the options include using 50¢ per degree or $1 per degree. This example works well using $1 per degree.

It would be beautifully simple if the $85 opening price—which translates to 85 degrees or 25 Gemini—were obviously marked in Google's horoscope. It is not—which is the first indicator pointing to the fact that $85 was never going to be an important level. The shares were launched at this price but have never returned to it. Had the $85 initial IPO price been significant, we ought to have found planet activity at or very near 25 degrees of Gemini (85 degrees from 0 Aries). The table above has no planet listed near this area of the zodiac.

It is, of course, possible to "dig deep" and discover facts

about this degree. Vesta (the trading asteroid) is at near right angles to this position. 25 Gemini is the midpoint of Jupiter and Vesta—a perfect "trading" combination. However, given that so much sleuthing is required to correlate $85 with the planet positions, it is unlikely that this price will have much relevance in Google's long term trading history—as has been the case.)

The chart shown on page 162 of Google's share price since the IPO shows the share price to have risen to as much as $740. From launch the price soon rose above $180 correlating with the Moon and Ascendant degree areas. It also made an important low at $256.

As we are now embarked on historical astro-analysis we need to calculate from price to time. This is not always immediately straightforward. Certainly a price of, e.g. $150 would convert to a planet positioned at 150 degrees or 0 Virgo and a price of $256 to 256 degrees or 16 Sagittarius.

But what happens when the given price is considerably over $360? In such instances we need to subtract multiples of $360 to bring us to a figure that resonates within the circle, i.e. less than $360.

Google reached a high of $741 on November 6, 2007: a meteoric rise of over $200 from the previous high of 547 reached mid July 2007. We begin by translating these prices into degrees of the zodiac.

$741 is greater than 360, so we must first subtract multiples of 360 to bring the figure to within the zodiac circle. In this instance, we must subtract twice (360 x 2 = 720). Our calculated figure is then 21—or 21 Aries. The closest planet position we have for this is for the Vertex at 14 Aries. The previous high was at $547—translating to 187 degrees—very close indeed to the Ascendant and Moon degrees of, respectively, 185 and 188. The low of $260, "translates" to 20 Sagittarius which is within one degree of Pluto's position at the IPO.

Let's imagine now that we were extremely cautious astro-traders disappointed that we had not bought in at the start and made a profit as Google reached $540. Encouraged though by clear evidence that the stock price was indeed responding to this simple planet price method and observing the upward momentum, we might reasonably deduce that a turning point would be at the Vertex price point: 720 + 14 ($734). Even the most cautious astro-trader—perhaps waiting until the price was close to $700, might have bought shares in anticipation of the price heading toward $734, and taken profits as soon as the price was near that figure. True, the stock went a little above this. Even so, the astro-trader would have made a profit

An astro-trader, focused on a particular year (2007) when key progressions took place, would have considered the positions of the slower moving planets (Saturn, Uranus, Neptune and Pluto) to ascertain the aspects each would make with the First Trade chart.

The impact of a Pluto transit on any chart is considerable. As Pluto moves so slowly and as, when viewed from Earth, can appear to occupy the same position three or five times, the effect of a Pluto transit (its aspects to the natal or progressed positions) takes place over a number of months. Pluto is used to identify a half-year period of singular activity. The faster moving planets are then used to narrow the time frame to weeks and then days.

Looking back to the original chart we see that at the IPO, the Sun position was 26 degree of a Fire sign (Leo) and that Pluto was at 19 degrees of another Fire sign.

When the July high of $540 was reached, Pluto's relationship to the Sun position in the IPO chart was almost exactly a third of a circle (120 degrees): Pluto was then at 26 Sagittarius and conjoining the Galactic Center so giving it further positive emphasis. If studying the chart of an individual experiencing a similar transit, an astrologer might talk of a period of empowerment. The same was always likely to be true of Google stock.

As we can see from the trading graph, GOOG stock declined after the Pluto trine aspect became exact: a not uncommon phenomenon. Through the following weeks Saturn was moving toward the Sun's IPO position, reaching this location on August 9, 2007. The Sun's degree position is 26 Leo: representing $146 or (adding 360) $504. The price did indeed touch this level before turning upward once more. As we shall see, given an approaching and highly unusual planetary formation set to be exact on November 7th, the astro-trader would have been able to

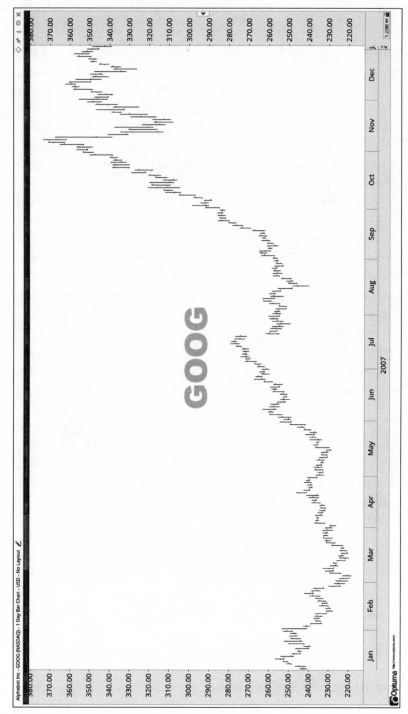

Alphabet- Google 2007

take advantage of this move by purchasing at this apparent low in August.

A Grand Trine of Mars-Uranus-Sun could be regarded as rare. Mars and Uranus are in trine with each other for approximately two separate weeks during any 26-month period. For the Sun to be in 120 degrees from both planets is highly unusual. This then is a distinctive and positive combination. Though this planet picture would be experienced by the whole market, the conjunction with Google's natal Venus hinted at the probability of a high being reached on November 7th at this Grand Trine. To add emphasis to the likely importance of that day, the Moon would also return to its position in the IPO chart.

Having determined that this date would probably bring a high, the big question would be what would the high be? The astro-trader would make note of the various points above $540 that might be reached. Included in this list would be Venus at 11 degrees of Cancer (101 degrees and accenting a price point of $821 [101 + 720]). Technical analysis would no doubt rule this level out. However, the Vertex level might well be reached at $734 (720 + 14).

The Vertex together with the Ascendant and Midheaven are peculiar to the exact location and time that a stock is launched. It makes sense that they should hold special importance for a stock and gives the astro-trader price points to note.

As may be seen from the graph, the price fell immediately and sharply after November 7, 2007. Again this is not unusual: once a major planetary configuration is passed, energy is lost.

Assuming that the astro-trader took profit at the high but retained interest in this stock, attention would then turn to an optimum purchase period. For this, the astro-trader would likely look for a significant Saturn (depressive) transit. Saturn formed a right angle to natal Pluto ($259) on November 19, 2008—the exact low.

Generally, astro-traders look for aspects which are multiples of 15 (24th of a circle), 30 (12th of a circle), or 45 degrees (an eighth of a circle). In looking for a depressed period, the astro-trader takes account of Saturn's transits particularly: noting those dates when Saturn will be 45 degrees (or a multiple of 45 degrees)

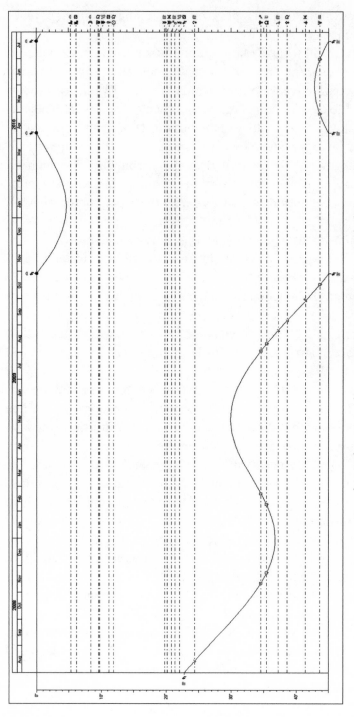

Graphic Ephemeris showing Saturn transit to natal Pluto

from natal or progressed positions. Such aspects tend to coincide with periods of headline-hitting eventfulness.

The accompanying graph (opposite) covers November 2008 through early 2010. We observe that Saturn is not clear of the Pluto position until August 2009. It was in August 2009 that Google shares recovered to what must be seen as a resistance level around $445. This is fascinating as $445 is $360 + $85— the original IPO price.

Our studies need to encompass the two-for-one share offer on April 12, 2012.

There is little doubt that the experienced astro-trader or astrologers would have identified this date as being of major significance. In the initial IPO chart, Mars lies opposite Uranus across the Virgo-Pisces axis. In 2012, Uranus was in mutual reception with Neptune.

The term "mutual reception" describes a situation where two planets are each moving through a sign preferred by the other. Uranus is said to rule Aquarius and Neptune, Pisces. In 2012, Uranus transited Pisces as Neptune transited Aquarius.

Implied sensitivity to the Mars-Uranus cycle as indicated by the IPO chart, could then manifest as sensitivity to the Mars-Neptune cycle during the Uranus-Neptune period of mutual reception. On April 12, 2012, Mars opposed Neptune within a degree of the Mars-Uranus natal axis: an event that had not taken place during Google's previous trading years.

The high following this event took place almost exactly six months later on October 5, 2012. This date marked Saturn's Scorpio ingress (translating to probable activity around price points of $210 and its multiple of $570. An ingress by Saturn or any of the slow-moving planets can be seen to mark an important shift in attitude on trading floors. Since Saturn does not change sign every year, the dates when an ingress takes place should be given particular attention.

On Monday, August 10, 2015, Google and its allied businesses announced that they would become part of a new holding company "Alphabet" on October 2, 2015. This announcement was made just as Jupiter made its Virgo geocentric ingress. Recall that the IPO chart for Google has a stellium in that sign and that Jupiter passes through Virgo just once in every dozen or so years. It might reasonably have been anticipated that as Jupiter moved through this sign, there would be signals of major development.

The links between the IPO chart and Alphabet's incorporation on October 2nd are many. It must be remembered however that in looking at these links we are comparing an IPO with another kind of entity: an incorporation. The two have decidedly different functions. Though cross-referencing is a fascinating and rewarding exercise, only one of these charts (the IPO) yields information about the share price. The chart for incorporation tells us more about the management and aims and objectives of the business.

The fact that there are strong links between the two charts is of interest, as without these, the effect of fresh incorporation could have resulted in share price stress. As we can see, the opposite occurred: Google's share price has increased, touching $775.96 in December 2015. This share price "translates" to $55.96 (55.96 + 720 = $775.96). $55.96 lies between 25 and 26 Taurus. There is no natal planet at this degree or in square or opposition to it.

This price most likely relates to a position in either the secondary progressed or solar arc directed chart. These positions are in constant motion and describe the developing price. The experienced astro-trader, watching the share price increase following the new incorporation would be looking for the next top to resonate with a position in either the progressed or directed chart. Given that any move would be in response to trading excitement, he or she might well have focused on the Directed Part of Fortune position at 26 Scorpio: directly opposite the 25–26 Taurus sensitive area.

Noting that the next level after this Directed Part of Fortune position would connect with a planet positioned in one of the Mutable signs (Gemini, Virgo, Sagittarius or Pisces) where it would either be conjunct, square, or in opposition to the planet position—and having weighed up the probability of this occurring against general market trend—this trader might well have concluded that taking profits a little early, say at $760 or so, would be acceptable.

Google's share price has consistently been above $360. To

determine the scale to be used per zodiac degree, we had several options: $1, $2, $5, or $10. Making the choice of $1 per zodiac degree was simple—my preference. In the case of other companies, where share prices are significantly lower, other scales would be used: one choice being 50¢. This latter scale might be used where the share price is not expected to rise above $180.

Example 2

WALMART

The choice of scale is personal. In the case of Walmart, I have chosen to use 25¢ per zodiac degree. Since its first trade, Walmart's shares have not risen above $90. Ninety represents a quarter of a circle so it is reasonable to use a quarter dollar for the scale. Had Walmart shares ever reached above $90, I would most likely have opted to use 50¢.

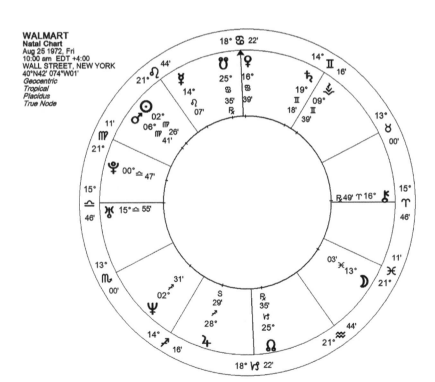

WALMART
Natal Chart
Aug 25 1972, Fri
10:00 am EDT +4:00
WALL STREET, NEW YORK
40°N42' 074°W01'
Geocentric
Tropical
Placidus
True Node

The first task is to convert each planet position to price points. As with Google, a simple approach is to find Aries on the chart and list the positions (moving counter clockwise) from this sign. We then arrive at this list:

Descendant:	15 Aries	Price point 3.75
Chiron	16 Aries	4
Vertex	10 Taurus	10
Vesta	9 Gemini	17.25
Saturn	19 Gemini	18.75
Venus	16 Cancer	26.5
Midheaven	18 Cancer	27
Mercury	14 Leo	33.5
Sun	2 Virgo	38
Mars	6 Virgo	39
Pluto	0 Libra	45
Ascendant	15 Libra	48.5
Uranus	15 Libra	48.5
Neptune	2 Sagittarius	121
Jupiter	28 Sagittarius	134
Node	24 Capricorn	147
Moon	13 Pisces	171.5

Walmart was offered for launch on August 25, 1972. This date is neither a Solstice or an Equinox or the half way point between them. As explained, First Trade launches coinciding with these powerful days in Earth's year, often give extra boost to shares launched on these dates.

In this instance, the Sun was in an early degree of Virgo and would, within days, form a conjunction with Mars: immediately suggesting the probability of active share price movement. That same day, Jupiter was passing close to the Galactic Center suggesting the potential for expansion. At the very moment of First Trade on Wall Street, Uranus was rising and shared the same degree as the Ascendant. Uranus occupies this position at opening of trade on Wall Street on just a few days every year. Uranus is the planet of "doing things differently" the net effect suggesting a stock that would stand out from the crowd with the potential to increase in value.

Students will find it an interesting exercise to trace Walmart shares over its long history. For the purposes of this chapter however, we will focus on the high of $89.26 reached on January 23, 2015. Recall that the scale used is 25¢ per degree. $90 then represents a complete cycle of the zodiac: the very end of Pisces and beginning of Aries. As we are also interested in 90 or 180 degree aspects to this, we would also consider planet positions on the Gemini/Cancer, Virgo, Libra, and Sagittarius/Capricorn borders. This draws attention to Pluto's position at 0 Libra.

At this stage we are in the process of "back-testing": we now need to know if there is any reason at all as to why Pluto's position should be accented on this date. It is, of course, pleasing to know that the planet involved is Pluto: one of the "Gods of Wealth."

The low took place on October 16, 2014 at 73.23, another figure unlisted above, and to which we must also add a multiple of 45. This gives a figure of 118.23: tantalizingly near the Neptune (loss) figure. Allowing for fluctuations during the trading day, the Neptune line was touched almost exactly.

If we are going to make use of this particular time and price method, then we need to know why these levels were so important on those dates. If there is a satisfactory explanation, then we can then go on to make forecasts and, perhaps, offer a trading strategy.

The "answers" are interesting. The January date came between Saturn's square to the Natal Sun and Pluto's square to the Progressed Sun. These aspects usually point to management change and leadership upheaval, and would certainly suggest pivotal change. Looking closely at that period, Vesta's conjunct to the Node might have stood out as a possible time to take profit.

The previous October, Uranus by transit opposed the natal Sun on the last day of that month, forming a trine with Mercury on the day of the actual low.

The astro-trader would certainly have been aware of the potential for dramatic news in October and would not have been surprised by the sudden low that month. There would have been expectation of volatility until Uranus had completed the opposition to the Sun—which might have been considered an optimum time to purchase.

These same traders would then be looking for dates on which to take profit: possibly arriving at the conclusion that with the upcoming transits by both Saturn and Pluto to the natal and progressed Suns respectively, that they should look for a suitable date in January (possibly taking into account their own chart).

Please note that although there was resonance with both the Jupiter and Neptune lines, there were no prominent aspects to either planet. The astro-trader is interested in the price points that can be determined from planetary positions—not necessarily aspects by transiting planets to those points.

What then for the future? In April 2017, the transiting Node conjuncts the Sun and two weeks later, Jupiter conjuncts the natal Uranus. This promises to be a period of marked (probably upward) activity. Indeed, it may be that Walmart stock bucks the anticipated negative trend as Saturn crosses the Galactic Center. This might not be the case later in the year however when, in December, Saturn conjoins natal Jupiter. This important transit draws attention to Jupiter lines. In combination with technical analysis and show a downturn be apparent through November, it should then be possible to determine the likely low.

Example 3

GENERAL MOTORS

The most recent IPO chart for the reformed General Motors is set for November 18, 2010, at 09.30 EST, Wall Street.

The scale used here is 1¢ for each degree. As before we check the chart and then list the various planet positions followed by the related price point.

Moon	19 Aries	19	1.9
IC	22 Aries	22	2.2
South Node	3 Cancer	93	9.3
Vertex	10 Leo	130	13.0
Saturn	13 Libra	193	19.3
Midheaven	22 Libra	202	20.2
Venus	27 Libra	217	21.7
Vesta	22 Scorpio	232	23.2
Sun	26 Scorpio	236	23.6
Mercury	14 Sagittarius	254	25.4
Mars	15 Sagittarius	255	25.5
Ascendant	29 Sagittarius	269	26.9
North Node	3 Capricorn	273	27.3
Pluto	3 Capricorn	273	27.3
Neptune	25 Aquarius	325	32.5
Chiron	28 Aquarius	326	32.60
Jupiter	23 Pisces	353	35.3
Uranus	26 Pisces	356	35.6

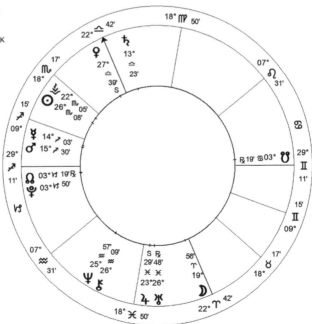

GENERAL MOTORS
Natal Chart
Nov 18 2010, Thu
9:30 am EST +5:00
WALL STREET, NEW YORK
40°N42' 074°W01'
Geocentric
Tropical
Placidus
True Node

Note that the Ascendant in this example was in a very late degree of Sagittarius. By direction, the Ascendant would move to Capricorn within weeks of the IPO. This fact alone would have alerted the financial astrologer to the probability of a sharp move in the share price: which proved to tbe the case.

From an IPO of $33, the stock rose to $38 in January 2011. Note first that $38 is not on the list of planet positions translated to price. It is, however, 180 degrees for Venus' line (217 + 180 = 397 or 360 + 37).

The interesting thing here is that Venus, proud in the chart by virtue of its position near the Midheaven is involved.

The financial astrologer, having witnessed this move would have noted the high probability of $38 becoming a sensitive price point: especially as the Midheaven would progress to this point within a few years from IPO.

The Midheaven is at 22 Libra and Venus at 27 of that sign: a difference of five degrees. Using either the standard method of progression or by directing by solar arc, the Midheaven conjoins Venus a little under five years from IPO. We should expect a price associated with Venus to be reached around this time. In fact, $38 was reached in March 2015.

Using the solar arc system, we also note that Venus would move from Libra to Scorpio in 2013: another year when significant activity around a Venus' level price would have been expected. In December 2013, the price reached $41, reflecting Venus' Directed position (+ 180).

A low of $19.73, in October 2011, marks both Moon and Saturn lines. The two are not in exact opposition in the IPO chart but sufficiently close in price point (Saturn at $19 and the Moon at $1.9 + 18: Moon + 180 degrees). In fact, this $19 has marked several lows since then and has been breached by only a few cents. It may be a highly significant price line. It is interesting to note that in October 2011, Saturn was transiting in exact opposition to the IPO Moon.

Following that exact transit on October 19th, Jupiter moved to trine the Midheaven on October 28th. As might have been anticipated, the price rose between the two events reached

$26.45. This price represents 90 degrees from both Jupiter and Uranus.

The financial astrologer would have noted that Saturn was moving to the IPO Midheaven (exact on November 3rd) and that Pluto would reach the Directed Midheaven two days earlier. The combination of events would certainly have alerted this trader to the high probability of another significant turning point being reached. This proved to be the case. The $26.45 level did not hold and the price then fell, recovering by February 6th of the following year but surpassing $26 to reach the exact Pluto and North Node point of $27.34 on February 17th.

Since that time, GM shares have fallen to an all-time low of $18.8 in late July 2012 (within orb of the Saturn line).

Research having shown evidence of correlation between time and price, we can now look to the future. In 2019, it will be nine years since the IPO. Directed Saturn will then be at the IPO Midheaven. In the charts of individuals whose solar arc directed Saturn arrives at the Midheaven within their working lives, career advancement is often seen. In the case of a stock, we might also hope for a peak to be reached.

Technical analysis would need to be used alongside astro-techniques. What might be anticipated is that price levels would, in some way, be related to the IPO Midheaven position and price point ($20.2). A possible level would include $20.2 + 90, ($29.2)

The study of IPO charts from the perspective of time and price is fascinating and can be of great use to the trader.

No less important is a review of the chart of the Chief Executive of the company. Though the actual time of birth might not be known, it is usually possible to determine the actual date of birth. Using this information and noting forthcoming connections with eclipses and major planet transits and, of course, the important Progressed Moon in Declination, further information comes to light.

Statements from the CEO of any company can affect the share price hugely. When the date of the Annual general Meeting is known, it is possible to have some idea if the CEO's statements will be optimistic or not.

Two final thoughts: conscientious investors will study a company's prospectus before making their investments. A review of the position of the planets at the company's end-of-year financial accounts is worthy of consideration. Presently Neptune is passing through Pisces, and at the end of each February is not far from conjunction with the Sun. Corporate year ends, occurring 6 months later in August, will have a year end chart with the Sun opposing Neptune. Years in May or November show the Sun in square to Neptune. Though many factors should be taken into account, it is entirely possible that figures are not as accurate as might be expected, requiring potential investors to investigate further.

With some companies (such as Google-Alphabet above) there is direct correlation between time, price, and planet position. This is not always the case. Discrepancies might be due to the scale in use. This does not nullify the system. What is important is that periods of likely significant activity are identified.

A BRIEF NOTE ON PROGRESSIONS

SOLAR ARC PROGRESSIONS
In this system the chart is progressed allowing the Sun's motion each day following birth as being equivalent to one year of life. This motion is then added to the natal position of the Moon and each planet. In consequence it takes the Moon or a planet approximately 30 years to travel through a sign.

SECONDARY PROGRESSIONS
A chart is calculated for each subsequent day following birth with each day marking one year of life. This 'day for a year' method results in the Moon changing signs approximately every 30 months.

Both forecasting systems have merit and can be used together.

CHAPTER NINE

YOUR OWN CHART

Clearly any exploration of the financial universe should include a review of one's own chart. A whole book could be written on this subject alone. For now, this overview may be helpful. There are no serious case studies included here, but I present a few case "snapshots" of experiences and incidents from my case book that are thought-provoking, even if they are not definitive research conclusions.

A recurrent question from clients is, "Does wealth show up in my chart?"—an obvious question but not one that is easy to answer:

True, it has long been recognized that certain signs appear more disposed toward material success than others, yet it is possible to find rich people born under every sign of the zodiac. For that reason I am disinclined to say that any one Sun-sign is "better" than others. It should be borne in mind too that much depends on the actual generation into which a person is born. Different generations experience different "background" influences from the slow moving planets, e.g. Leos born in the 1950s have faced different challenges than those of other generations.

What does seem to be important is the position of the Moon at birth. Clearly not everyone is born at New Moon, when the Sun and Moon are together in the same sign: it is more common to be born with the Sun in one sign and Moon in another. Where the Moon was at your birth can be found from a variety of sources. All that is needed is the date and time of birth. Again, no single sign seems "better" than another though I am sure it helps if the Moon is in good aspect to either Venus, Jupiter or Neptune. These people seem to have a knack for tuning in to abundance and attracting it.

Of course, this begs the question of what is counted as "good." Generally, conjunctions, sextiles and trines are viewed as having positive influence. The same might also be true of quintile and septile aspects—whereas divisions of the circle by eight bring tensions that some describe as being negative and unhelpful.

To clarify this a little more: the Moon is said to "work" better in Cancer and to "not work as well" in Scorpio. Yet it is not true that those born with the Moon in Scorpio will all experience either bad financial fortune or show signs of poor money judgement: other factors can and usually do compensate.

Although it has been suggested that those with the Moon in aspect to Mars, Saturn, or Pluto—or in "bad" aspect to Venus or Jupiter—attract "bad" fortune, this is not my experience. To me it seems that these individuals have a different kind of financial focus—they seem to need to apply considerable effort to achieve success. For some of these individuals, it appears that financial success is permanently "beyond reach" and that they must endure hardship (which they often attract as a result). Yet it is not uncommon for individuals with these apparently difficult aspects to be hugely successful—though agreed, they work long and hard to realize that success.

I have not studied thousands or even hundreds of charts, but what I have noted is that a serious liability for creating and maintaining wealth is when the Moon is positioned at 29 degrees of a sign. Those who have the Moon at 28 degrees of a sign should not worry as my observations suggest that it is only when the Moon is in the very last degree (29 degrees) of a sign that problems appear insurmountable. Please note that I am not saying that these individuals will not experience periods of substantial financial recompense and success. The difficulty seems to lie in holding on to this and in building reserve to cover lean years.

One client with exactly this placement, has, on three occasions in the last decade, secured funds several times the national average wage in his country. On each occasion, he has managed to go through this money in a matter of months. True, some of the cash has been used to pay off debts. Even so, there ought to have been enough money left to cover a few years of living expenses. Despite having a well-placed Saturn, he does not appear to have good regulating ability.

Perhaps it is the case that when the Moon is in the apparently weakened position of 29 degrees of a sign that the language and vocabulary of the individual is geared toward announcing lack or insufficiency. This habit may be so ingrained that "lack" becomes the norm. In the case of my client, he appears to enjoy the pursuit of large gain and the dialogue and negotiations necessary to achieve this, but has not—as yet—found a means of regulating funds when they arrive.

Though few are born with the Moon in these late degree positions, everyone will experience periods in life when the progressed Moon passes through the last degrees of a sign. Actually, at least two forecasting techniques: Progressions and Directions identify periods when this will be the case. My experience with clients to date suggests that these are not favorable times for financial activity. In the case of the Progressed Moon (direct or converse), there is a six-week period every 18–24 months when even the best of financial thinking goes awry.

An explanation of these techniques is given at the end of this chapter. Some readers may prefer that an astrologer calculates these for them.

When employing the Directed technique (based on Solar Arc), once the Moon reaches 29 degrees of a sign, it will then be approximately three decades before there is recurrence. Each time the Moon holds this position however, there is strong likelihood of approximately a year of financial trickiness. Using the Progressed Moon technique—where the Moon moves through a sign approximately every eighteen months—there may be significant cash flow challenges for a few weeks, whereas with the Directed Moon, problems are likely to last for around 14 months.

Clients and students have asked: "Does my chart show if I will make money?" I am not sure that there is a single answer. It does seem to be the case that certain aspects show up frequently in the charts of those who attract wealth. I doubt if sufficient research has been done on this and so prefer to talk about how various aspects might be used to attract wealth and good, financial fortune.

Horoscopes are usually divided into twelve houses or

segments. To confuse matters, this division can be calculated in many different ways. A standard method is to use the Ascendant degree and mark off every 30 degrees following this. This is known as an Equal House system. While not perfect, it does yield interesting results. It is not my preferred system but neither do I ignore it given that that it gives great weighting to the Ascendant and the individual's relationships. As important for me is the division of the horoscope in 30 degree units from the Midheaven. Using this system it is possible to determine career paths, developments and, from my experience, plot financial progress.

It is generally recognized that the 2nd, 5th, 8th, and 11th houses of a chart (using whatever system) are relevant to financial matters. It is absolutely NOT necessary to have the Sun or Moon placed in one of these to assure financial success, though it is probably true that if the Sun or Moon is in one of these areas, there is greater likelihood that the individual will give significant attention to financial matters and build wealth as a result.

Though it is sometimes suggested in textbooks, I am not sure that those who have Neptune in one of these houses will experience lack. It perhaps more likely that they have an assumption that all will be well financially which—dependent on other factors—can bring them into difficulty. They may be seduced into thinking that all is well when insufficient attention to practicalities results in everything being far from well-ordered.

Neither would I necessarily view Saturn in one of these areas as a financial curse. It is more likely that these individuals feel the weight of fiscal responsibility keenly. A good example here is of someone born with the Moon in the 8th house who, at their Saturn return (around age 30), received a legacy. Welcome and timely as this was, it did require her to learn about stocks, shares and dividends. Lacking this expertise and, after a few years of trying, but unwilling to continue these studies, she handed her portfolio to someone older and very experienced (how Saturn!) who now manages investments on her behalf.

TRANSITS TO THE NATAL CHART

Aside from natal positions, transits must be considered. Saturn takes approximately three decades to tour the chart. Within that time-frame it will spend periods in each of the "financial" houses. My observations are that great care should be taken not to acquire debt ahead of Saturn transits through these areas. I can think of instances where mortgages have been agreed when Saturn was moving through the 1st, 4th, 7th, and 10th sectors of the chart and where the individuals involved have been comfortable with the contract. Saturn then passes on to the 2nd, 5th, 8th, or 11th and either interest rates have risen or the client's income has been reduced. As a result, Saturn's passage through the financial houses has been ultra-challenging—in once case leading to default just as Saturn was concluding one of these passages, and in another, where the person managed to hang on through tricky times, renegotiating the debt as Saturn moved into the 9th house.

Discussions about how to have debt levels at a minimum before Saturn enters the 2nd, 5th, 8th, or 11th houses has proved helpful to the client. Future planning is based on more than preparing for Saturn transits however.

For many people, discontinuity in financial matters usually occurs when Uranus by transit, progression or direction accentuates a planetary picture. Astrologers often give examples of shocking events that led to financial chaos or calamity. Some, dealing with an upcoming Uranus event might even venture to suggest putting a safety-net in place so as to be prepared for any eventuality.

It does seem to be the case that when Uranus transits through the financial zones of the natal chart, unstable cash flow is experienced. A rough and ready reckoner may be used: if we assume that the person's life-span will match the 84 years that it takes Uranus to complete a cycle of the zodiac, then for a third of the life-time Uranus will be moving through one of these zones. A rhythm can be mapped. Let's suppose that Uranus was on the Ascendant at birth. Roughly seven years later it will begin to transit the 2nd house. Fourteen years after concluding this transit and leaving the 2nd Uranus will enter the 5th house: beginning another seven-year period of instability. That rhythm will then repeat twice. Rarely does the life-rhythm work out in exactly this way however. For some people a transit through one house may be significantly longer than another.

Bumpy as the financial ride may be when Uranus is at work, it may not be all "bad" news: these same periods can also bring tremendous financial success even if at the outset there is complete shock and bewilderment at events.

My experience has been that Uranus is the "planet of the entrepreneur." Those with this planet accented in the natal chart will either develop their own business or develop a profitable second revenue stream. Uranus demands fresh perspective, and is a hugely creative if demanding force. An excellent example of someone who tuned in to Uranus' vibration was Anita Roddick, founder of the Body Shop. Her autobiography *Doing Business Differently* sums up her approach.

Entrepreneurship and Uranus fit together easily. Even so, success requires that Saturn too is at work. Few would disagree that Uranus' genius is one thing but that the diligence, persistence and hard slog required to turn a creative idea into profitability requires extraordinary self-discipline.

Those well-suited to carving their own niche in the business world often have Uranus at one of the angles in their birth chart or in strong aspect to their Sun or Moon. These are the people for whom self-employment works well—though the degree of their financial success will depend on Saturn's position both in the natal chart and in transit, and, obviously, the inter-relationship between Saturn and Uranus.

The sheer unpredictability that comes with financial structures built on Uranus' vibration can certainly bring financial ruin. Even excellent products or services require capital until the concept is "off the ground." A classic example is someone running a market stall, doing really well with an original idea or concept, taking out a loan in order to transfer into an apparently suitable shop but then finding that they don't have enough stock or insufficient capital to sustain the business.

"Start-up" companies are usually begun by those with a "great idea." The accompanying incorporation date charts are important. As crucial however are the time, date and place of the first transaction. This is when the company really gains life and energy—though agreed, the potential for this to occur is usually shown in the inauguration chart.

THE CHART OF A BUSINESS

Astrologers put considerable energy into determining what they think is a suitable date for launch or incorporation: they rarely have control of that first sale however. My experience suggests that in selecting a date, considerable attention must be given to the position of Uranus and any applying aspects involving this planet.

Here I would like to offer a working example: a long-established and successful company was owned by a gentleman who felt he had made his fortune and wanted to retire. He was happy to sell out to the managers of the four stores that he had developed. Each store was wholly viable on its own. The four managers each had strong Uranus aspects: involving the Sun and two the Moon.

This was in 1989 when Saturn and Uranus were conjunct and at the start of their new cycle. A year later, and at their first annual meeting, with Jupiter opposing Saturn, they made the decision to expand their product range. Loans were sought and approved. Each of the four businesses continued to thrive: overall profits were good. Insufficient effort however was given to either reducing debt or building a sound cash reserve. On top of this, the banks at that time were only too keen to lend more money. The directors, flush with apparent success and confidence in a growing economy, decided to expand and open two more stores.

The greatest expansions took place between the Jupiter Saturn conjunction of 2000. By 2005 the group was breaching credit limits and the possibility of defaulting on loans began to dawn. At this point, the partnership, perhaps predictably, broke up. The two directors with the Sun Uranus aspects in their natal charts went on to develop singular but smaller enterprises. These are still in existence a decade later.

The two directors with Moon Uranus aspects did not fare so well. Both have since been made bankrupt.

THE INFLUENCE OF NEPTUNE

As stated earlier, some feel that Neptune in the second house of the chart is not good news for money matters. I haven't seen so many charts with Neptune in this position but have been struck by a particular trait: the individuals concerned are constantly hopeful that a flow of cash is headed towards them. In some cases, that has proved to be the case. In two cases however the opposite manifested. As Saturn transited their second house Neptune position, both experienced extreme lack and, at least for the few months that Saturn was passing this position, total disillusionment and the sense that dreams could never get off the ground simply because they had insufficient financial capital.

Yet I have also had the experience of someone with Neptune in the second house in trine formation to her Sun. When Saturn passed this position and trined her Cancerian Sun, she developed a solid property portfolio which has brought her great wealth.

As we know, Neptune moves very slowly. Since the early 1990s, it has been moving through the signs of Capricorn, followed by Aquarius and Pisces. The Sun is in these signs from December 21 to March 21. Businesses and individuals whose year-end falls within these dates will, at some point, have experienced the Sun conjunct Neptune in their end of year accounts charts. My experience to date has been that with each business whose year-end has concluded with Sun conjunct Neptune, the accounts have later proved to have been factually incorrect. In one case profit was overstated and in two others, significantly understated.

As it takes Neptune 146 years to travel through all 12 signs of the zodiac, no individual experiences what would be called the "Neptune return." At best, Neptune will only travel a little more than halfway around the chart: perhaps as few as six houses of the chart. Neptune cannot pass through the 2nd, 5th, 8th, and

11th houses of an individual's chart, but is likely to pass through one or two of these.

Tempting as it might be to suggest that these periods will bring financial loss, and particularly if Neptune makes hard aspects to key planets or points in the natal chart, this is not always the case. Indeed, from the investment point of view, Neptune passing through these areas though not attracting immediate wealth, can be beneficial in the long term.

Even the apparently difficult transit of Neptune in hard aspects to Jupiter, though not at all easy to negotiate at the time, can bring positive developments later. I have one client who, under exactly these conditions, and with Neptune moving through her fifth house, began working on a cruise liner. Her job was to look after the jewellery boutique on board. As Neptune squared her Jupiter, extra cash gained through commission seemed to disappear as fast as it was earned. As the transit came to an end, she was showered with bonuses.

It is worth mentioning that it is under Neptune transits that many creative ideas develop. Henry Ford, founder of the Ford Motor Company, designed and brought to market his original black sedan. While working on the car, he presumably had no thought of the wealth that he would later acquire. The car was created under a Neptune transit to his Mercury. I have no idea if anyone has ever quantified the number of hours put in toward his initial creation. In keeping with the keywords we associate with Neptune, time was fluid and the task took as long as it took.

These days, when realizing that a client is about to experience a long Neptune transit, I mention the Ford story. Obviously, other factors in the chart have to be given due consideration. Yet it seems to me that Neptune's presence, either by transit, progression, direction, or even in the natal chart can bring a stream of abundance.

THE INFLUENCE OF PLUTO

Slow-moving Pluto can spend a decade or more in any of the houses but never completes an entire circuit of the horoscope (which would take approximately 246 years). In contrast to the Sun which transits the natal chart every year, Pluto makes few aspects by transit. These tend to bring periods of high drama—perhaps not entirely unconnected to the fact that there is no earlier experience on which to draw.

It is certainly true that there are case histories showing dramatic events when Pluto conjoined—exactly—natal planets or key points of the chart. Pluto, though, is "God of the Underworld" and there are as many instances when it seems that a Pluto transit has passed unnoticed only for its effect to be revealed later. Further research shows the initial incident to have coincided with mathematical precision as Pluto made aspect to a sensitive point in the person's chart. An example is given below.

Discernible impact seems to be most keenly felt as Pluto enters each new house or sector of the horoscope. Where financial matters are concerned, I have noted two definite effects—one that correlates with Pluto's entry into each house as calculated by the Equal House system, and another correlating with Pluto's entry into that same house as calculated using the Placidus House system. A common theme has been that taxation matters have required attention.

From my experience, Pluto's transit to the Ascendant has brought about significant but essential financial readjustment. True, this has been connected with changes in close partnerships. In the cases I have studied, it has also required some tax management. Pluto's transit to the opposite point—and also to the Vertex (two cases)—coincided with career changes and with the need to master unfamiliar accounting operations.

Pluto's crossing over the Midheaven required an individual to review his tax position with regard to inheritance planning, while a transit to a Sagittarius IC required that person to learn about overseas tax management.

A transit of Pluto to an 8th house Moon correlated with what became a quite extraordinary story. In this chart, the Moon ruled the IC. One possible manifestation concerned legacies. Nothing appeared to happen. There was no major event. The person did not move. There was no change in the partner's position.

It appeared for a long time that the transit had passed without incident.

Nothing could have been further from the truth—though the financial impact of this transit was not understood until Pluto was on the 9th house cusp and when an archiving project brought to light the "missing incident."

An item had been bought just as Pluto made its second transit (there were three in all) to the natal Moon. It was not bought as an investment and actually required annual payment to ensure its ownership. Products and services not initially linked to the investment were gradually brought together. By the time Pluto reached the 9th house cusp, valuations and taxation required attention. At this juncture it became clear that significant value had accrued and that a fresh financial approach would be required.

GAMBLER'S CURSE ASPECTS

If I am wary of any single transit when dealing with financial matters it is the transit of Jupiter opposing natal and progressed Pluto. As Jupiter travels through the zodiac approximately every twelve years, we all experience this transit a few times in a life time. Sadly any lessons learned at one of these transits seem to be forgotten when the transit recurs a little over a decade later.

Jupiter and Pluto are, respectively, Kings of the Heavens and the Underworld. Humans cannot survive without the nutrients provided by both. The problem is that when Jupiter takes up opposition to Pluto, the individual often feels it's OK to play at being a god too. As a result, unwise decisions are taken. At the very least people pay over-the-odds for items or get locked into interest rates that are too high. Though the transit itself may be over in a matter of weeks, its legacy can be long-lasting. My experience suggests that this is not a good time to trade unless you are highly, highly experienced. The temptation to take a risk too far is great.

The trader under this aspect is cautioned to pull him or herself back from the brink. When the transiting planet is Pluto—

and when this planet opposes natal or progressed Jupiter—pulling back from the brink (again only my experience) does not seem possible. There is a compulsion that cannot apparently be denied.

Let's first consider how many people will experience this transit. During the course of a lifetime, Pluto, which takes nearly a quarter of a millennium to pass through all twelve signs, will only cover a fraction of the zodiac. If you were born in the 1980s with Pluto in Scorpio and live until you are 100, then Pluto will travel through a little over 180 degrees—perhaps as much as seven signs of the zodiac. Only those with Jupiter in their opposite sign will experience Pluto's opposition to Jupiter. Almost half of those born at a similar time but who don't have Jupiter in these signs will be spared this transit.

As explained, Pluto moves slowly so that it can hold position opposite natal Jupiter (and the progressed Jupiter) for many months—almost two years in some cases.

It is normal for Pluto to bring a degree of uprooting. In this instance, not only are there likely to be tax problems—which may well require legal services to resolve—but there is also the danger of the individual taking hefty risks.

I can think of two cases where the effect of Pluto opposing natal Jupiter has offered excruciating financial lessons. In the first case a property carrying a very large mortgage was purchased as Pluto was a few degrees away from natal Jupiter. Interest rates rose, it became nearly impossible to service the mortgage and only through grim determination and considerable sacrifice, did the person manage to hang on in there and not lose the roof over the family heads.

In the second case, a trader who usually excelled in trading USD/GBP, came unstuck when Pluto opposed Jupiter EXACTLY. He lost a considerable amount of money and compounded the error as Pluto opposed progressed Jupiter a little later. Recovery from these losses took some considerable time.

What was interesting was his description of what happened through that period. Even knowing that his logic and technical trading skills were malfunctioning, he said he felt compelled to continue: effectively increasing his "bet" and therefore his losses through this period.

I am not sure where or when I learned the term "gambler's curse" but suspect it was at a lecture given by the superbly talented astrologer Charles Harvey back in the 1980s. Trading clients respond well to this term and, I like to think, financial calamities have been avoided through advising them of this inclement personal trading weather.

PROGRESSED MOON

A reliable financial rhythm can be discerned by using the position of the progressed Moon in declination. This system has one major positive feature: that the actual time of birth is not needed to create a useful diagram. The graph is drawn assuming the individual will live for 100 years. In each case, ups and downs are seen. Tempting as it may be to assume that the top of a curve marks an "uplift" and its accompanying low point as being a "dip" in affairs, this is generally NOT the case. Though some astrologers feel that one turning point is better than another, my experience suggests that they are one in the same. For my colleagues, friends and clients, these periods have brought crisis which, in most cases, has also brought significant change of financial direction.

My approach is to discuss this graph with the client. The graph can be used to review the early part of someone's life. Often clients cannot remember anything from their early years but, from age 18 onward interesting information can be found. The norm is for an event (usually a domestic shake-up) to have taken place just ahead of a turning point. This then leads to the need to make further changes which are often expensive. It can take up to a year after the turning point for the financial situation to stabilize. Note that this entire exercise can be done WITHOUT using the position of natal, progressed or directed planets. However, once these are placed on the graph, interpretation takes on greater depth.

No two individuals are the same. Likewise, there are whole groups of people whose turning points coincide with parallel aspects to outer planets. An example would be those born in the early 1950s, when both Uranus and Pluto were in parallel. Those falling into this group do not all experience the same crisis, but a common factor may well be rising interest rates or changes in tax regulations that prompt them to group together to, perhaps, place a class action.

Clients will, of course, be keen to know where they are at that moment on the curve and are usually relieved if they find that they have just negotiated a major turning point. This, quite naturally, puts them in very positive frame of mind. Where I know that a client is just going into a dip, I tend not to show the graph until she has told me more of her story and I have considered other factors.

If one of these turning points is some years ahead, I usually make suggestions about building a reserve so as to be prepared for what could prove a stressful period.

It seems too that as the wave moves over the 0 degrees point another—but sometimes, subtle—change of financial gears takes place. So far my experience suggests that when the wave is moving upward (the Moon moving from South to North declination) a second revenue stream begins to flow. When the curve is moving downward at 0 degrees (North to South declination) then increased attention is given to investments. As explained however, I have not reviewed hundreds of charts!

Following this exploration of the Progressed Moon in declination, we move on to look at the Moon's Progressed position. Here, the relationship between the Natal and Progressed Sun and Progressed Moon, and between the Progressed and Natal Moon must be given high priority. What we are look at here is usually a question of attitude. This is particularly important when the individual is going through a period of apparent lack. It may be that a negative vibration is at work. Discussing this, the possible duration of the feeling and how best to mitigate it can be hugely helpful. It can be the case too that looking back on a similar period in the past, and the "walls of resistance or strength" that were built in the individual's memory bank at that time, can be explored and either reinforced or knocked down entirely.

Periods of abundance—weeks or a full year—depending on whether the Progressed or Directed Moon is being used, tend to occur more when Venus, Jupiter, Uranus, or Pluto are involved. Where these aspects echo those in the natal chart, there can be obvious attraction of wealth.

As might be expected, where the lunar link is to Mars or Saturn, it is perhaps easier for the individual to feel pinched or restricted through lack of cash. Again, if this is a reflection of a natal aspect, e.g. Moon opposing Saturn, the individual can feel truly crushed or oppressed. People at this point are unlikely to be willing to discuss Laws of Attraction or Abundance, feeling rather more at home with discussing the probable duration of impoverishment.

PART OF FORTUNE

Where the exact time of birth is known, it is possible to calculate the positions of what is commonly known as "Pars" or the "Part of Fortune." To calculate this requires knowing the exact degree of Sun, Moon, and Ascendant. Two formulae for its calculation are recognized: one for a day-time birth and the other for a night time birth.

Venus, which moves through the entire zodiac during the course of a year will cross this point annually (though not always on the same date). There may occasionally be years when, thanks to Venus moving retrograde, Venus crosses the degree concerned more than once. Jupiter will transit this position at least once every twelve years and sometimes, thanks to retrogradation, three times in a matter of months.

When these transits occur (and again note that this is not based on a vast collection of data), there has indeed been a financial break-through and, in my own case, a successful horse-racing bet.

The progressed Part of Fortune should also be considered. So far I have found this to be a compelling point to study. Holding position for approximately one month, and with a favorable Jupiter transit, I have seen this bring a period of good fortune. I note too that when a normally highly successful trader's Progressed Part of Fortune was conjoined by Saturn, it seemed that he was incapable of making a good trade.

Independent of the natal chart, the Part of Fortune, like the Ascendant and Midheaven, moves throughout the course of the day. Though much more work needs to be done, it does appear that when Jupiter aligns with this degree during trading hours, there is a spike in volume of trade—usually pushing prices upward.

TRADING

Not everyone is suited to trading. For some people it is better to leave investment to experts. Yet some people appear compelled to take part in commercial transactions. Note that this is not always the same as trading the markets. I worked with one extremely shrewd business woman who would never have thought of trading stocks, commodities, or foreign exchange—but had no difficulty whatsoever with import and export markets. Another is gifted in the property market. Both have the asteroid, Vesta, as a prominent feature of their charts though in neither case is the asteroid on an angle.

I have found it fascinating to discover that so many of the traders I have worked with have the asteroid Vesta in a prominent position. By this we mean that Vesta is at one of the angles of the chart, or in conjunction to the Sun or Moon. Please note that I have not studied thousands of such charts. It may be that I have attracted only those whose Vesta is in these positions. Even so, I think it a noteworthy factor.

There are some, who though they do not trade themselves, are fascinated by the idea and who, with training, might excel. These individuals have Vesta conjunct Pluto. Of this group, those born with the two planets in Virgo seem particularly well equipped especially when they combine astro studies with technical analysis.

Mathematical ability plays its part. My experience suggests that promising trading ability requires a planetary signature with prominent Vesta, as well as Mercury and Saturn in good aspect (including the quintile).

YOUR FINANCIAL ADVISOR

For most people, their financial advisor is as important as their personal physician. Finding the "right" advisor can be a challenge. It is rare to find someone who understands perfectly one's needs. In the course of my work I have met three professional financial advisors whose attention to detail has been exemplary and who have counselled well. Though not born in the same year, they share one key planetary combination: Vesta's conjunction with Neptune. Two have this conjunction in Libra while the other has the conjunction in Scorpio. No doubt they take different approaches. What they share is an ability to hold long-term vision and to tune in to the often unspoken needs of their clients.

One other interesting theme here is that they have each told me—in a relatively obscure way—about issues they experienced with the media and film (Neptune) industry. Though they have been less than specific—and have given proper attention to client confidentiality—they have each intimated the difficulties of speculating in this area where each seems to have come unstuck. Astrologers will have little difficulty in understanding the symbolism here. It appears that these three individuals—despite their undoubted skill elsewhere—have been seduced into thinking that investments in this sector would work well. For them it appears these investments have failed.

Last word in this chapter should go to the intriguing case of another client who, during her working life, never once traded but who, when put in charge of her partner's pension pot, was more successful than she imagined. Please note that she did indeed make errors of judgement but that her choice of investments, the strategies she used, and her diligent research proves her to be an able trader. In her chart, Vesta squares the nodal axis.

CHAPTER TEN

LOOKING AHEAD

Pluto's Capricorn ingress in 2008 coincided with what has been labeled the "global financial crisis." Pluto does not leave Capricorn (the sign associated with banking, large institutions, and governments and countries) until 2024. Since that time, the number of wars has increased. Many borders are under threat and it is to be expected that by the time Pluto enters Aquarius, the world political map will look very different.

The years 2018–24 could be markedly different from anything we have yet known. While it is reasonable to expect developments in science and technology, most of us would prefer not to hear the drumbeats of war. Yet if history repeats—and correlation between planetary cycles and human behavior is as I suggest—then those incessant drumbeats cannot be ignored. Before Pluto leaves Capricorn in 2024, we may yet witness an escalation in worldwide hostilities. The drum beats of war, already in evidence at the time of writing, will surely increase in the coming years. It is unlikely that they will diminish before Pluto moves into Aquarius in 2024. Until then, the reinforcing and, perhaps, redefinition of borders are the dominating features of the next few years. It is probable too that Phase Two of the global financial crisis will affect the bond market.

This conclusion is reached through analysis of solar, lunar, and planetary cycles. Attention in this chapter is given to an overview of these years with more detailed attention given to 2017–22 in the next and final chapter of this work.

THE SUN, MOON, OUTER PLANET CYCLES, AND WEATHER

As we saw in an opening chapter, the sunspot cycle has an average length of 11.2 years but can be as long as 14 years. Cycle 24 began with solar minimum in 2007–08. It is possible that minimum could occur as early as 2017 (if the cycle is a short one), but is more likely to occur between 2018 and 2022: years during which major planetary configurations are also set to take place.

While the Sun's gravity holds the planets in their orbits, the planets themselves have an effect on the Sun. As explained in an earlier chapter many planets will be grouped on one side of the Sun in 2020. It may be that the planets "pull" the Sun toward them, so creating solar wind disturbances that eventually give rise to ever greater disturbed terrestrial weather systems. Throughout Solar Cycle 24, the number of sunspots has been significant lower than those of earlier cycles: a factor in the climate change experienced in recent years. The concentration of planets on one side of the Sun in 2020 could bring further weather chaos—quite independent of the expected disturbance correlating with solar minimum.

This "pull" on the Sun may also see the rise in the number of outbursts of coronal mass ejections (CMEs). These could bring significant magnetic disturbance with the potential to affect satellite systems. Given our dependence on communications and GPS systems using these orbiting masterpieces of technology, governments would be well-advised to give attention to risk management should outages occur.

The role of the Moon must be added to this picture. The Moon's position relative to Earth causes changes in air pressure and water temperatures. Those studying lunar cycles, i.e actual perigee and apogee and their interaction with the Solstices and Equinoxes, have noted that the position of the Moon in 2020 will be similar to that of 1901 when Australia recorded its worst ever drought. If history repeats, then the East side of that country will be seriously affected through 2019–20.

Nor is Australia the only country likely to suffer: across South East Asia especially, and with perhaps, lack of monsoon rains, crops will be damaged. In the Americas unusually high levels of rainfall could decimate normal crop productions.

El Ninos occur, on average, about twice per decade and follow solar cycle peaks and minimums. The next El Ninos should follow the expected solar minimum in 2020–22. If the El Nino of 2015/16 is anything to go by, then the early part of the next decade should see an increase in warm air current, subsequent increase in rainfall and, yet again, the high probability of flooding in certain parts of the world.

In June 2018 and again in May 2019, Uranus and Neptune will be an eighth of a cycle apart. It is a curious "coincidence" that when a major angle between these two planets forms during the crop-sowing period part of any year, the Mississippi river floods. A contra-parallel aspect between the two formed in May 2016. Note that flooding took place in late December 2015 and the early part of 2016, ahead of exactitude of the aspect, but as the Moon was in perigee. A repeat could occur in late 2018/early 2019. The May 2019 aspect—a semi-square or eighth of a circle—is particularly worrying in that hard aspects between the two planets have resulted in terrible flooding in the past. Severe devastation in the region could occur. Whether in S.E. Asia, Australia, or the USA, there is high probability that destructive weather patterns will lead to an increase in the price of many crops.

90 YEAR CYCLE

In 2019, it will be exactly 90 years since the Great Crash of 1929 and 45 years since the stock market losses of the early 1970s. These numbers are of great importance. W. D. Gann made much of the division of a circle by first two, then four, then eight, and interpreting the resulting number of degrees as a number of years. His argument that these numbers have relevance is compelling. Using this division of the circle by 4 or 8, we ought to anticipate a global slump in equities toward the end of the present decade. Perhaps only the fittest of companies will survive. That statement may also be true of countries. In recent times we have begun to accept that countries can experience bankruptcy. We should expect more instances of national financial collapse between 2018 and 2024. Given the chronic levels of debt apparent even now mid-way through the second decade of the 21st century, we ought not to be surprised that so many countries teeter on the edge of financial disaster.

As has been noted elsewhere in this book, the position of

the outer planets in 2020 presents a rare alignment. The last time that Jupiter, Saturn and Pluto moved together through the sign of Capricorn was in 1285. They do not come together in this sign again until December 2754.

As we know, history never repeats EXACTLY. Yet the themes of a particular period are often replayed. In 1294, there was a credit and financial collapse in Europe prompted by kings defaulting on debt accrued in previous years. From 1294 to 2019 is 725 years—a little over two complete cycles. Gann would almost certainly have allowed a little margin here and would surely have anticipated the theme of credit collapse to dominate sometime around 2014. Noting the 90 years from 1929 and the 45 years from 1973, he would surely be expecting major credit challenges around 2019.

Even this is only part of the story. Toward the end of the 13th century, many currencies were operating in Europe. These were eventually reduced to just a few (the Florentine Florin being the main beneficiary) post the financial collapse of that period. Already it seems that there are similarities between that earlier period and the present.

Since the banking crisis of 2007, many new currencies have come to market: e.g. Bitcoin, ChinaCoin, Feather coin, etc. Some of these "virtual" or cypto-currencies, are developing new forms too, e.g. BitGold. All this is happening at the same time as cash is losing favor. In the UK in 2014, just 48% of retail trade was done using cash. That proportion is expected to drop further in 2015 as contactless cards become more widely used.

As Pluto completes its transit of Capricorn, we should expect Capricorn (banking systems) to come under increasing duress. The sign following Capricorn is Aquarius. New crypto-currencies may be linked to this sign. Bitcoin was launched with a stellium in that sign. It is to be expected that by the time Jupiter and Saturn form their next conjunction (in Aquarius) in 2020, that considerable attention will be given to these currencies which could enjoy growth through 2021–24. Once Pluto arrives in Aquarius in late 2024 however, the potential for corruption and manipulation of these markets may well result in the sudden demise of several these young currencies.

The growing use of debit cards and the advent of these new currencies demands secure computer systems. Already there have been instances where these systems have been out of action causing—at the very least—inconvenience and, for some, hardship. Banks here in the UK have had to compensate those affected. The advent of contactless payments may be exciting, but the systems operating these must be robust: something that may be impossible to create and maintain.

Gold is not as revered in Western cultures as it is in the East. It may well be that it is the peoples of the East who will drive the price upward in the coming years. At the time of writing, the gold price is at $1180. Its price is likely to soar—perhaps reaching 4 times this level before the end of the decade as those who lack confidence in new systems turn to systems that have stood the test of time. The position of the planets in 2020 suggests growing confidence in these "old" currencies which will surely be reflected by higher prices for gold in particular.

In October 2012, geocentric Saturn moved into Scorpio and gold prices fell. Saturn is often viewed as a depressant, and with Scorpio the sign associated with the underworld, perhaps this was not so surprising. Jupiter reaches this sign in October 2017 however and with this could come the first signals of the price reviving and then exceeding earlier values.

Aside from any loss of confidence in young currencies, another driver that might well lift gold could be Saturn's transit over the Galactic Center in 2017, when investors, turning away from stocks, will choose to invest in this apparently safer form of exchange.

GOLD STANDARD

On August 15, 1971, President Nixon of the United States announced that dollars would no longer be convertible into gold. The shock announcement coincided with Mars conjoining the lunar North Node in Aquarius. Rather more importantly, Uranus (planet of the unexpected) was at the midpoint of Jupiter and Vesta. The combined effect says much about a change of attitude toward trade. From the heliocentric perspective, Saturn and Pluto were EXACTLY a third of a circle apart. It may be that this planetary "chord," which speaks of a profound administrative development, was as important as those geocentric aspects.

The next question must surely be, "Could there be a return to the Gold Standard?" and does the 1971 chart give clues as to when this might take place.

One possibility is to review the heliocentric picture. Both Saturn and Pluto were then in Earth signs. Since then, and though the two have been through an entire cycle (conjunction to conjunction) and more, each phase has been in any other element of the zodiac than Earth. It is only in 2020 that the two will once again accent the Earth element when they conjoin in Capricorn.

If this is indeed the key to a "Gold Standard code," then we need to find a date close to their 2020 conjunction when Uranus is once more at the midpoint of Jupiter and Vesta. This gives just two possible dates: February 18, 2019 and October 19, 2020. Of the two, the former is arguably the stronger candidate, as on that date not only is there a Venus-Saturn conjunction in Earth (Taurus), but the actual position of this opposes Ceres' position in the 1971 chart. *True, Saturn has opposed this position before but not alongside Venus.* Perhaps as importantly, both the Sun and Uranus are about to change sign. The Sun will be moving to Pisces, and Uranus, having made its Taurus ingress but then retrograded back into Aries, makes its final crossing into the Sign of the Bull.

WAR

The issue of debt is likely to be the focus of considerable attention at the end of the present decade. Just as quantatitive easing methods were used in 2008, new systems for the repayment of debt will surely need to be found.

Yet supposing a "can't or won't pay" stance prevails? Undoubtedly there would then be an escalation in war, and the acquisition or attempted acquisition of countries or land grabs.

Developments in the Middle East, as Uranus and Pluto formed their square aspect between 2010 and 2015, brought many countries into a local conflict. While these two planets do not repeat this aspect in the next decade, they form a latitude contra-parallel in October 2017 and a parallel in September 2019. This may be experienced as echoes of that earlier conflict but could also coincide with other outbreaks of war.

Many planet cycles can be linked to war, with the Uranus-Pluto cycle perhaps the most dominant. Coming a close second however must be the Saturn-Pluto cycle—and especially when one or the other planet is moving through a zodiac sign in which it is said to work well. This is the case in 2020 when Saturn and Pluto conjoin.

To recap: Saturn and Pluto form a conjunction every 45 years, Jupiter and Saturn every 20 years, and Jupiter and Pluto every 11 years. It is unusual however for these conjunctions to coincide within the space of a little over a year—as they do between 2019 and 2020. In apparently sharing the same zodiacal area, they give emphasis to both the sign involved, Capricorn, and to a particular degree area: 22 degrees of that sign.

At the December Solstice 2020, Mars and Pluto are in square to one another with Mars in Aries (a sign in which it is said to work especially well). Mars and Pluto offer a violent energy. Mars will be on or near the Ascendant in various capitals in the Middle East, while in the USA, Mars is close to the apex of chart and Pluto is on the Descendant. The possibility of "flare up" in the Middle East involving the USA seems great.

Yet a different kind of hostility could appear within global financial systems in the coming years and may be linked to another important cycle.

CHIRON AND NEPTUNE

In this second decade of the 21st century, Chiron and Neptune separate from a conjunction formed in 2010. Chiron, the faster moving of the two, will move into the sign of Aries (2018) ahead of Neptune by roughly six years.

Their conjunction took place on February 17th, 2010 and, geocentrically at 26 Aquarius. As we have seen elsewhere, planets appear to have stronger influence as they move through certain areas of the zodiac than they do others. Neither Chiron nor Neptune works particularly well moving through Aquarius with which neither has particular affinity. Chiron, arguably, works "best" while moving through Virgo where its problem-solving abilities are put to the test, while Neptune apparently works best as it transits Pisces. At their conjunction, the vibration of each may be tangled and confused with outcomes uncertain and, in practical terms, perhaps even dangerous.

While the February 2010 date marks the moment of their exact mathematical alignment, the two were already drawing ever closer together from 2008.

One definition of Chiron conjunct Neptune would be "papering over the cracks." In the wake of the global financial crisis, many countries chose to adopt financial solutions that were equivalent to the printing of cash. In very few cases have the debts of nations been truly addressed. True, some may feel that decisions taken were imaginative. They were surely also full of unknowing-ness: desperate events to keep the global financial system running. A return to a deep depression similar to that of the 1930s was deemed unthinkable, and unprecedented actions were taken. Quantatitive easing may have been thought of as cool and logical (words linked with Aquarius), but it is as likely that a maze has been laid and that the escape route from colossal debt is and was unclear from the start.

Chiron and Neptune opposed one another across the 12 Cancer-Capricorn axis in 1990. It is entirely possible that what are now described as weapons of mass financial destruction developed at a fast pace from that year, and that only as these two bodies came into alignment in 2008–10, was the full reality of their corrupting influence realized.

History records the actual date of their most recent conjunction as the day when French wine-makers, angered at certain American producers producing what they termed "fake French wine," prepared for legal battle. Words such as "fake," "malformed," or "corrupt," and "weakened" are entirely in keeping with the mix of Chiron and Neptune. Aquarius—the sign associated not with legalities but with debate and logic, is noted as being the sign most associated with "taking a stand."

It is interesting to look back at the early part of February 2010 when Chiron and Neptune conjoined, and to assess the strength (taking a stand) of financial decisions at that time. From late in 2009, it was clear that some states within the Eurozone would be unable to repay their debts. The led to the European Central Bank offering two temporary rescue schemes both of which have been used to support Greece, Portugal and Ireland. These facilities were later extended to Spain and Cyprus.

As we now know, even this was not enough to secure their financial stability. Though each country has dealt with the situation differently, the process of resolution has proved painful for both the peoples of the various nations and their governments. The political landscape in each of these countries has changed dramatically.

Through 2020 and 2021, Chiron and Neptune are in contra-parallel aspect with the former moving through Aries and the latter transiting Pisces. A strong possibility is that yet more "temporary" solutions to the debt crisis will be discussed. It is as likely though that these will require painful (Chiron) cuts (Aries) to services provided to many (Neptune in Pisces).

No cycle is "all bad" however: there is little doubt that since the Chiron-Neptune conjunction, advances in both biochemistry and in media-related technologies have been considerable. Consider the burgeoning number of apparently problem-solving, (Chiron), easy access (Neptune) apps that have become available in recent years.

"Insidious" might also be used as a keyword for this cycle. Though many developments have held us spell-bound, it is also likely to be true that a genie has escaped from the bottle and that without regulation, there is very real danger of corruption taking on impetus. Consider: we now know more about genetic coding than ever before. Companies offering linked services have sprung up almost overnight. The data they hold could yet be used against us however. Exciting as it may be to know that body parts can be "regrown," this could pave the way for malicious action.

Attention to these matters will surely become urgent and vital as Chiron moves from Pisces to Aries.

CHIRON

Chiron makes its Aries ingress in 2018. As any planet (or planetoid in this case) moves from one sign to another, it seems that human-kind responds by acting and thinking differently. Chiron, discovered in 1977, is often described as the "wounded healer" and certainly can be shown to hold a key position in the charts of those working in the field of medicine. Yet as we have seen, Chiron should also be viewed as a problem-solver—coming from the base line of experience. In financial terms, Chiron may be seen as auditor: not accountant or financial advisor, but the person whose task is to assess the position at any time, presenting risk analysis where necessary, and considering not just the final profit and loss position but also the goodwill or otherwise built over time.

Chiron entered Pisces in 2010. As with the crossing of any slow-moving planet into a new area of the zodiac, inspiration in industries associated with the sign involved was apparent. The sign of Pisces has association with all that is fluid, viscous, often unquantifiable, and apparently magical. Pharmaceuticals and hospitals are viewed as "Piscean" as are the oil and alcohol industries, as well as football, dance, ballet, and optics.

Amongst the many developments since that year, understanding of genetics has increased and, with it, medical breakthroughs and advances have been made. At the time of writing, and where cancers are concerned, tailored treatments that take account of a person's genetic makeup are now available. In other areas too, bio-diversity is better understood. Of course this is not all "good" news. There are very real concerns as to what the genetic modification of crops will mean for the planet as a whole. As is so often the case, the Chiron effect demands focused understanding of the down-sides.

The magical, playful side of Pisces is at work in the many apps available for tablet and phone devices. Yet there is a negative side here too: subliminal advertising is felt by some to be a corrosive and corrupting influence. Companies working within each of these areas have much to contend with as Chiron moves through Pisces yet are also making spectacular gains in the process.

Chiron traveling through Aries is likely to be dramatic in a different way: making it clear that in many areas, the cutting-edge is sharp (an Aries word). Chiron last transited this sign between 1918 and 1926 and again between 1968 and 1976. As always there are multiple themes that may be said to connect the two periods. An obvious one concerns the media and local media systems. Connecting those who are experiencing difficulties to those who can solve them at speed is probable. There may be significant growth in small local companies offering physical response systems. A neat image for Aries is of Tarzan: physical, strong and there when needed.

Of course, advances in the field of medicine are unlikely to stop when Chiron leaves Pisces. As this planetoid moves on into Aries, its influence will surely be felt—but rather than through cell structure or drug manufacture, through fast, key-hole surgeries. Present MRI machines are large and cumbersome. With Chiron in Aries, these machines are likely to be developed into highly portable machines so cutting the time from diagnosis to restorative action and care.

Pisces is often associated with minutiae and as Chiron moved through this sign, attention has been drawn to the need for there to be computerized channels that deal with micro-payments that have been a boon to many. At a different level, trading strategies that bring gains by moving money within fractions of a second have developed as well as alternative currencies backed by nothing tangible whatsoever. As always, there have been "good" and "not so good" developments.

Focusing on the world of finance, Chiron's Aries influence is sure to focus on speed: Aries, is, after all, both a Cardinal and Fire sign. As with the sent email which you would like to call back, the speed at which transactions are carried out—at times in error or even unlawfully—is sure to be of growing concern. The scale of some of these transactions could even result in some systems coming near to collapse.

It is interesting that though Chiron is in Aries from 2018 to 2024 as Pluto is in another of the Cardinal signs, Capricorn, they do not form an exact square with one another until 2028—by which time both will have moved into Fixed signs of the zodiac. Though the angle never forms exactly before 2028, there are other midpoint factors pointing to the probability of the two working together between 2018 and 2024. In this respect, the stage for drama is likely to be the bond market. Indeed, putting various factors together, it is entirely possible that one rogue movement could topple the bond market which some would argue is already in a fragile condition. It may be that the Saturn-Pluto conjunction of 2020 is the backdrop for this calamity.

Another, and serious possibility, is that those who have been manipulating markets will be called to account. It may then be found that much has been over-valued: again setting the scene for de- and re-construction.

It is worth noting that Saturn is on the Chiron-Pluto midpoint in December 2018 and the Lunar Node is in square to this midpoint on October 2021. Though total collapse might yet be averted, the fortnight around both dates should see significant levels of stress in bond markets.

BLACK HOLES

So far we have given consideration to the role of the Sun and the distributions of the known planets around our special star. We have also touched on the role of the Galactic Center which also happens to be a Black Hole.

Black Holes, or collapsed suns, consist of extraordinarily dense matter: so dense that even light cannot escape. The Galactic Center is not the only Black Hole with the potential to affect life on earth in the coming years. Enormous energy is locked within each of them. There is another Black Hole at 22 degrees Capricorn. With all three planets, Jupiter, Saturn, and Pluto aligning with this

Black Hole in 2019 and 2020, it is possible that these planets will act as transmitters. We cannot know to what extent this might affect Earth but, if recent alignments with the Galactic Center are anything to do by, it is probable that the world will be touched by some form of calamity.

It seems likely that the passage of Pluto over 22 Capricorn will be felt keenly and experienced as a deep, deep, throbbing beat resonating across the universe. One of the great proponents of the influence of Black Holes and other Deep Space objects is Alex Miller. He states that the influence of a Black Hole makes any apparent influence by Pluto appear infantile. If that is the case, then the end of this decade could witness catastrophe on a grand scale.

This is a bleak perspective. Influences from beyond our solar system are clearly beyond human control. It is, of course, to be hoped that none of the above comes to pass. Even if cosmic influences do not affect Earth in this particular way, it seems likely that the passage of Pluto across this sensitive area of Capricorn will coincide with financial debacle: one possibility being that governments across the world will be faced with the very real problem of how to deal with accumulated debt.

THE SATURN FACTOR

Saturn's role should not be underestimated. It is often thought of as the planet of limitation and contraction. Yet it can also bring periods of tangible reward for effort. Each business sector is said to be "ruled by" a particular planet and has affinity with a zodiac sign. As might be expected, as Saturn moves from one area of the zodiac to another, it draws attention to weakness or potential for specific sectors or companies.

Between 2018 and 2024, Saturn moves through just three signs of the zodiac: Sagittarius, Capricorn and Aquarius. It is said to work efficiently in (is ruler of) both Capricorn and Aquarius. As we have seen, its arrival in Capricorn coincides with the Winter Solstice in 2018. Its Aquarius ingress coincides with another Equinox (March 2020) and, later in the year, its complete ingress (after being retrograde for some months), within days of the December Solstice and its conjunction with Jupiter.

When Saturn enters Capricorn, it is the turn of politicians, economists, and bankers to be called to account. Though some could receive excellent reports, those who haven't done the appropriate "homework" will surely be asked to "stay behind" to explain themselves. Between late 2017 and 2020 large institutions and corporations should find that they have much explaining to do to investors—especially if their share prices have fallen more than the average during the expected downturn as Saturn crosses the Galactic center in 2017.

As Saturn makes its way through Capricorn and aligns with Pluto, the death knell for some businesses—including those with household names may be heard. Those businesses that came to market 90 or perhaps 135 (90 + 45) years previously, in 1929/30 or 1884/5, could be considered vulnerable. At the very least, a shake-up of their management structure, financial restructuring and, perhaps relocation is probable: likely affecting their share price if only temporarily. Large corporations with global network are likely to find business is severely interrupted by war. Many, even those thought to be indestructible, could crumble under the strain of both man-made (war) and natural catastrophe.

That said, and as suggested, Saturn can also bring reward for those who show patience, diligence, and determination: qualities easier to put into practice if debt is not a factor. Investors then should take a careful look at the strength of even the most apparently well-maintained Capricorn businesses through 2018 and 2019 and, perhaps, jettison those stocks likely to be found vulnerable.

The restricting and demanding influence of Saturn as it moves through Aquarius is likely to be experienced differently. For the first year of this transit, Saturn is accompanied by Jupiter: lessening the negative "pruning down" effect and suggesting cautious optimism for some global trades. Through December 2020–late 2021 and with Jupiter's benign influence in operation, developments in cutting edge technologies should be considerable. Again, those with a sound capital base (possibly secured through crowd-funding) ought to buck any downward trend in stock value and instead increase both their share price and influence.

One sector that ought to do well through this period relates to advances in space. Companies developing space technology and adventure should find that their products and services are much sought after, and that their share price grows in consequence.

THE POLITICAL LANDSCAPE

The extraordinary emphasis on the sign of Capricorn at the end of the present decade suggests a rise in support for right-wing parties—especially those shouting loudest about the need to protect and secure borders.

When Jupiter and Saturn arrive in Aquarius at the end of 2020 a swing in quite the other direction is probable. Aquarius is the sign of the "common man." This sign is associated with humanitarian operations and with non-government operations. Alternatives to present systems are likely to be demanded and found. It may be thought no longer necessary to have one person hold the votes of many: especially when it is recognized that the advances in technology used to harness political support could also be used to allow each person greater say.

The combined transit of Jupiter and Saturn through Aquarius could be seen as the overture to Pluto's arrival in that sign in 2024, when the overthrow of a large number of governments is probable.

CHAPTER ELEVEN

REVERBERATIONS AND FORECASTS 2017–2020

The forecasts which follow are built on observations of the apparent correlation between planetary formations and singular events in world markets: on the assumption that similar patterns will bring comparable reactions. Though events do not repeat exactly, there are many instances where, as we saw in earlier chapters, there is sufficient indication that history repeats.

2017

In 2017, Saturn returns to an area of the zodiac it transited in 1929, 1957, and 1987—all years recalled with some horror by those who study markets. In each of these years Saturn crossed the Galactic Center. Saturn moves over the sensitive 26–27 Sagittarius degree three times between February and May 2017. Through this same period, Pluto nears 19 Capricorn: an area of the zodiac that has also been present at times of dramatic, and negative market activity. This four month period should be regarded as difficult and demanding for all traders and investors.

At the beginning of the year, Jupiter and Saturn are in latitude parallel aspect: an aspect that recurs at the Summer Solstice on June 22nd and again on October 19th. This cycle is important: within the overall 20 year cycle (longitudinal conjunction to conjunction) there are minor cycles created by latitude and declination. These should each be viewed as periods of obvious and concerted effort to correct imbalance. As it seems likely that 2017 will be a year of marked volatility, it may be that the final low point of the year is not reached until the final latitude parallel aspect on October 19th. Indeed, if prices fall as expected, this may well be a significant buying opportunity.

It is normal for those using planetary-cycles as part of their arsenal of trading tools to give attention to the chart for the preceding December Solstice and also to the opening of trade charts of each stock exchange at the start of the New Year.

Whichever of these charts is used to make a forecast for 2017, the developing grouping of planets in Pisces that is particularly noticeable at the Full Moon of January 12th cannot be ignored. This concentration of planets positioned in Pisces could have significant impact on the NYSE.

In the January Full Moon chart, Venus, Mars, Chiron, Neptune, and the South Node are all moving through Pisces with Mars opposing its own exact degree in the chart for the inauguration of the NYSE. Closer inspection of that day—and using the chart set for the closing bell on Wall Street—puts Jupiter's opposition to Uranus in a prominent position. It may be that some traders will feel the market has gone "high enough" and that this sparks a minor sell off. Some traders may draw the conclusion that 2017 will not be a good year and choose to leave the market early or adjust their strategy to take into account declining stock values.

As suggested above, Saturn's position with regard to its cycles with other planets warrants careful consideration. It is clear that Saturn's transit of the Galactic Center degree coincides with decidedly negative market activity. Chiron did not appear as part of a major planet configuration in 1957, but in 1929 was an eighth of a circle from Saturn (semi-square) and in 1987, Saturn and Chiron were in opposition. In 2017, Saturn and Chiron are in square formation: part of this same sequence of hard aspects. This should put the astro-trader on alert as echoes of 1929 and 1987 may well be heard.

Saturn and Chiron together suggest that accountability and serious audit will be high priority. It is probable that exposed cracks in financial systems will widen to become documented and newsworthy fissures, and that those cracks will result in traders reducing the value of stocks. As if to prove the point, a brief look at the most recent Saturn-Chiron conjunction in April 1966 and a review of the Dow Jones index at that time reveals that market response to this cycle is truly negative. On April 13, 1966 (the exact aspect) the Dow Jones had a high of 945. Six months later it had lost over 200 points. We may conclude that following the conjunction, square or opposition of Saturn and Chiron, there is usually a stock-market decline.

Anniversaries of significant dates prompt memory and repetition of events. If Wednesday April 13, 1966 marked a top, then within days of the Full Moon of April 11, 2017, when Saturn forms a square to Chiron, a turning point may be reached.

Coinciding with Saturn and Chiron's alignment with the Galactic Center the Moon's North Node moves from Virgo to Leo (remember that the Moon's Node moves backwards through the signs). Nearly a century ago the financial astrologer Louise McWhirter offered the observation that this particular ingress marked a significant point in the (US) business cycle. At this point, activity is said to turn down having been in upswing through those years when the Node moved from Aquarius to and through Virgo.

Underscoring the likelihood of financial debacle through the early part of 2017 is another important aspect: the square between Jupiter and Pluto (sometimes known as the Gambler's Curse aspect.) This aspect should be given extra weight as Pluto holds the geocentric position of 19 Capricorn: a degree occupied at each of the stock market crashes of the 20th century.

The Full Moon of April 11, 2017 (shown on the next page and set for New York), certainly suggests drama. In this chart, the Sun and Uranus are in close conjunction in Aries, while at the other side of the zodiac, the Moon and Jupiter are within hours of their monthly conjunction. Between these conjunctions lies Pluto: so forming a Cardinal T-square. The total picture suggests the release of sudden (Uranus), large (Jupiter) power (Pluto).

Of course, it is possible that stock markets will be unaffected and that the Full Moon will instead bring natural disaster. Pressure on the Earth's crust may be considerable. Though planetary conditions are not identical to those of the Boxing Day Full Moon—that conjoined Uranus and fell between two Super Moons (when the Moon is at 90% or greater of its mean closest approach to Earth)—there may be evidence of Earth upheaval through earthquake, bush fire, storm or volcanic activity.

Nor do the cosmic clues for financial mayhem in early 2017 stop here: the period between the lunar (February 11th) and solar (February 26th) eclipses could be volatile. Markets do not always experience downturns at either kind of eclipse, though a

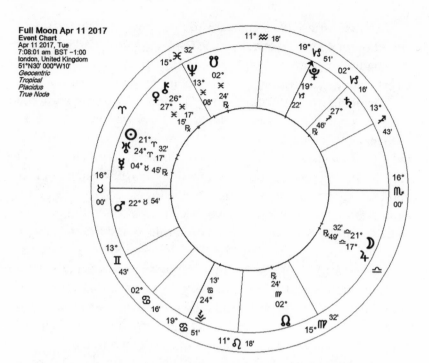

Full Moon Apr 11 2017
Event Chart
Apr 11 2017, Tue
7:08:01 am BST –1:00
london, United Kingdom
51°N30' 000°W10'
Geocentric
Tropical
Placidus
True Node

lunar eclipse has a tendency to coincide with downturn, usually apparent in the week following the event. This particular lunar eclipse is singular in that the Full Moon conjoins Regulus: one of the Fixed and Royal stars.

Note the order in which the February eclipses occur: the lunar precedes the solar. It is entirely possible that there will be obvious recovery by the solar eclipse, should markets decline on or after a market top at the lunar event. Strong moves between eclipses have occurred in the past: as in October 2014 when the Dow Jones Index fell four hundred points in the week following the lunar eclipse only to recover by the solar eclipse a week later. This bounce is not an unusual reaction to eclipses forming in this order—especially if the two events encompass a period when there is an ingress of the Sun or a planet.

As is common, when the Sun, Moon, or any planet moves from one sign of the zodiac to another, there is a mood shift. Thus if markets do decline as the Sun moves through Aquarius, then the reaction as the Sun moves on into Pisces should be the reverse (just as in October 2014, the Sun moved from another Air sign, Libra, to the Water sign of Scorpio).

Examination of the eclipses of 2009 when, as in 2017, Venus was retrograde, gives further clue as to potential market reaction: the March low of 2009 coincided with Venus' retrograde station and followed a lunar eclipse across the Aquarius-Leo axis. The Dow Jones index had lost over 2000 points from the lunar eclipse. If we look back to an earlier lunar eclipse across the Aquarius-Leo axis in 1999, we find that there were significant negative moves following that lunar eclipse also.

A study of Venus' movements in 2017 also suggest difficulties in the global marketplace. Over the course of eight years, Venus traces a pentagon shape with each point of the pentagon marked by a conjunction of the Sun and Venus. Venus then returns to the same part of the zodiac. The financial astrologer will find that this 8-year cycle a fascinating area of study. For example, Venus reaches maximum latitude in the first quarter of the year—as it did in March 2009. That proved a dramatic month for world share indices with most experiencing sharp falls—though not on the day of maximum latitude itself. The interplay between Venus and other planets highlighted the key date that year as March 9th. Once again we must look for interplay between planet cycles: in 2017, Venus conjoins Chiron and squares Saturn on April 8th, just two days after Saturn stations on the Galactic Center, and within just a few days of the aforementioned Full Moon.

Venus' retrograde movement in 2017 has the planet criss-crossing from Pisces to Aries and back again. The stationary points may be hugely significant. On March 4th, Venus stations at 13 degrees of Aries. In 2014, Uranus occupied this degree while Pluto was at right angles to it. This was within the long-term Uranus-Pluto square of 2010–2015 that witnessed considerable political upheaval worldwide. It is quite possible that March 4th 2017 will be significant in this respect and that "market memory" will ensure that between this date and March 9th (the 2009 anniversary) will prove to be a demanding time for traders.

Remarkably there is yet more evidence of sharp drops to be experienced in 2017. The very fine financial astrologer Arch

Crawford defined a "market crash cycle" noting the frequency of markets tops that correlated with significant phases in the Mars-Uranus cycle. These two planets reach their opposition phase on the day of the February solar eclipse: further evidence of the potential for a market top to be reached that month. The cosmic clues thus far suggest volatility between the solar and lunar eclipses in February with, quite possibly, a very sharp drop between the two events.

The asteroid Vesta's movements in 2017—especially in the first three months of the year also suggest the likelihood of volatility. This asteroid stations at 20 Cancer—within a degree of exact opposition to the sensitive 19 Capricorn degree—and in opposition to Pluto on March 7th as Saturn crosses the Galactic Center degree. That same day the Sun and Mercury at 17 Pisces reach conjunction—potentially marking another turning point.

As mentioned with reference to the Full Moon chart of January 12th, Mars is positioned at 17 Virgo in the chart for the New York Stock Exchange (NYSE). It has long been noted that as Mars, Jupiter, Saturn, Uranus, or Pluto pass this degree, strong market reaction frequently occurs. On March 7th (and so nearly the anniversary of the low marked on March 9, 2009), the Sun and Mercury oppose this degree, as Vesta opposes Pluto, and Saturn transits the Galactic Center. Equities could experience a low. As likely is a degree of mayhem in the currency markets.

The likelihood of there being marked reaction increases when consideration is given to Vesta's declination cycle. Vesta will be "out of orb," i.e. at more than 23 degrees declination. This extreme position could coincide with extreme reaction. Given that the Moon moves through Cancer that day, and that the charts for both the July 4, 1776 and the generally used chart for the US dollar are both affected, it may be that the US dollar is much affected: perhaps challenged by the Euro whose chart is also affected by major transits through this period.

Recovery after this date is probable, however, with another relative high likely to be reached mid-April, slightly ahead of the aforementioned Full Moon. All told, faint-hearted astro-traders could suffer in the first half of the year if their technical experience provides insufficient security. All the astro evidence for this period suggests marked volatility with potentially severe lows.

Markets though do not continue in a straight line, either up or down and there is some evidence to suggest a change of direction during the summer months. The Sun-Mars conjunction in Leo on July 27th may be significant. Research shows that from the last sextile of this cycle, and through to the conjunction (start) of the next Sun-Mars cycle, markets are energized and prices increase accordingly. If the past repeats, then July 27th should mark a minor high. Traders—if their technical analysis supports the theory—may choose to take profits around this date before returning to purchase when markets reach the expected low after the August lunar eclipse.

This lunar eclipse takes place on August 7th and, if history does indeed repeat, a short decline may be apparent during the week August 7th to 14th. The latter date—if supported by technical analysis at the time—suggests a buy signal. The August solar eclipse differs from its February counterpart. This solar eclipse is at 28 Leo: a sign often associated with the color gold and with gold itself.

With the Sun-Mars conjunction of July 27th also in this sign, astro-traders will surely have increased interest in the gold price. Study of the gold price in 2002 (the last Sun-Mars conjunction in Leo) reveals the conjunction to have coincided with a minor top for that year. This then became a level of resistance the following year. Certainly those with interest in this commodity should note the level reached on July 27th, as this is likely to be important.

Though the price is likely to fall from this date, the Leo solar eclipse suggests only temporary decrease in value. The probability of this is confirmed by a review of the Jupiter-Saturn cycle.

In October 2013 the gold price fell dramatically as Saturn made its geocentric Scorpio ingress. An opposite reaction seems feasible when Jupiter arrives in Scorpio on October 10th.

A commonly used technique is to note those dates when the planets cross the degree of the solar eclipse. Over September 2nd and 3rd, both Mercury and Mars make this passage suggesting that these dates will see resistance levels in gold and across markets generally being tested.

If gold prices do start to move upward, then the period November 8th through 13th could see a marked rise. Vesta opposes Uranus on November 8th while forming a trine aspect to Saturn. Again, if the past does reveal the future, then we ought to expect volatility in foreign exchange markets. There may be many whose trust in currencies: crypto or paper, is weak and so decide that they would prefer to hold precious metals instead. There is much to suggest an increase in gold prices that week.

Saturn will, by then, be leaving the all-important Galactic Center and be heading toward its Capricorn ingress. Note that this is the sign in which Saturn is said to work best. We should expect its arrival in this sign—which coincides with the December Solstice—to mark a moment of significant and singular activity.

As Capricorn is the sign associated with banking and governments, the Sun-Saturn conjunction and Capricorn ingress are likely to turn attention to government debt (bonds) and how these are to be repaid. Following the stock market difficulties of earlier in the year, politicians will surely be challenged to make statements that suggest they have matters under control. This though is unlikely and a painful period of austerity could be ushered in.

Another possibility is that some large corporations, angered by the rules, regulations and tax restrictions applied by some governments will announce plans to move to other jurisdictions. 2017 could mark the start of an exodus from the USA in particular to English-speaking countries where the rules are more lax and where corporation tax is much lower.

2018

Saturn transited Capricorn three times during the 20th century. Through that period there were four groups of conjunctions, with each group consisting of two or three actual conjunctions. One of those dates can be discounted as it coincided with Christmas Day. On several occasions however, the Dow Jones index rose in the weeks leading up to the Sun-Saturn conjunction and fell markedly in the weeks following it. There is little reason to suppose that the conjunction in December 2017 will be any different. Indices may well rise into this date but fall within weeks. The Full Moon of January 2nd that opens 2018 is promising in that it contains many positive aspects. Decline might not begin until after that date.

Strengthening the probability of a decline following the December Solstice is that in that chart, the Sun, Venus, Saturn, and Pluto are all in parallel aspect. The combined forces of Saturn and Pluto alone suggest the need to pare down and prune or—as outlined above—uproot and move to a new location. In this chart Venus lies close to the Galactic Center, prompting thoughts of serious (Saturn) and global (Galactic Center) activity. International taxation rules and regulations could come under the spotlight. In this chart too, Mars, Jupiter, and Vesta are all traveling through the sign of Scorpio. Real concerns about black-market activity could give rise to a call for draconian measures and international concerted efforts to combat illegal trade.

Since the global financial difficulties at the end of the last decade, few have been called to account. This Solstice chart suggests a very different attitude surfacing; with the likelihood of harsh penalties being placed on those who have apparently circumvented rules.

Further confirming the likelihood of a downward trend at the start of 2018, the lunar North Node will be within weeks of moving from Leo to Cancer. If the McWhirter cycle repeats, then a downturn in market activity is probable.

2018 opens with a Full Moon at 11° Cancer-Capricorn. In this chart, there is a Water Grand Trine between Jupiter, Neptune, and the Moon. Jupiter will be square the nodal axis. This combination suggests a tidal wave of activity that ought to see markets rise in response. It may be that after a year of difficulty, traders need to experience a swell of optimism. That optimism however is likely to be short-lived.

Markets should recover from the lunar eclipse at the end of January through to the mid-February solar eclipse. The Full Moon chart of March 2nd, contains promising aspects between Mercury Venus and Jupiter—so it may be that equities continue to rise from the solar eclipse into this lunation. The degrees involved in the Mercury-Venus-Jupiter combination connect to planetary positions in the charts of Microsoft, IBM, and Google and suggests an increase in their share price at this time.

However, the next Full Moon on March 31st could mark a significantly black moment. The chart has Saturn squaring both the Sun and Moon. If markets recover after the expected fall post the Sun-Saturn alignment, then this Full Moon should bring a severe downturn. That trend could start a few days earlier when Chiron makes a 135 degree aspect to the Lunar Node. Chiron will then be making its passage across the very late degrees of Pisces. The last degree of this sign is often cited as the "weeping degree." The period March 25th to 31st could see falling prices.

Companies most likely to be affected are those long considered to be "blue-chip." Indeed, it may be that many of these companies announce selloffs as they seek to divest themselves of those areas weakened by trading activity in 2017.

A change of pace is indicated by Chiron's move into Aries on April 17th, and enhanced by Venus' reaching out-of-bound status a few days later. Venus will be at maximum declination for the year on May 25th. Just nine days earlier, and as the New York Stock Exchange celebrates the anniversary of its inauguration, the Lunar Node forms parallels with the midpoints of Jupiter and Uranus, and Neptune and Chiron. Between May 17th and 25th, Saturn arrives at the midpoint of Uranus and Neptune by declination. As if this were not enough to reinforce the conclusion that this period in 2018 will see a rapid change in trading activity, the Full Moon on May 29th is dominated by another Water Grand Trine—this time between Venus, Jupiter, and Neptune. Uranus will also have made its Taurus ingress.

It seems entirely reasonable to suggest that May 2018 will witness a surge in stock market activity with sectors that have been in the doldrums moving quickly forward as demand for certain products and services increases. Those products and services will surely be linked to Uranus in Taurus. Taurus is one of the

Earth signs and, as we know, Uranus is linked to electricity and technology. This immediately suggests that companies providing safe and well grounded electrical equipment will increase in value.

It is equally likely that many countries will announce investment in dams, reservoirs and pumps as efforts are made to use water (the Grand Trine) wisely. Developments in hydro-electricity could also result in companies working in this area seeing the value of their shares rise as demand for their products and services increases.

Other sectors associated with the sign of Taurus include banking, savings and loans, securities, coins and general investments. Uranus' arrival in this sign suggests upheaval in these areas and an increase in the price of stocks offering alternatives to long established businesses and methods. As we saw in the chapter on currencies, it is probable that electronic methods of trading will increase.

This would tie in with another interesting aspect taking place from late July to mid-September. Through these weeks Vesta and Mercury form a parallel aspect. This cycle will be of special interest to currency traders. Mercury is known as the "planet of commerce" and, as we have seen, the asteroid Vesta often holds a prominent position in the charts of traders. Through these weeks then, fluctuation in currency values may well be considerable.

Away from finance, the sign of Taurus is associated with leather goods and with confectionery. With the former, we might expect that those companies that have made their name through providing excellent quality leather materials, will offer leather substitutes, where the difference between the substitutes and natural product is barely discernible.

It is probable too that there will be an increase in the number of products that can be used as an alternative to sugar. Scientific studies that show the health benefits of using these new products, rather than sugar, should also ensure significant demand and consequent rising share price.

It may be that finding alternatives to sugar is made imperative when crops fail to thrive as expected. The Full Moon chart for March 2, 2018, while containing what are generally regarded as positive aspects between Mercury, Venus, and Jupiter, also shows the Sun to be conjunct Neptune while opposing the Moon. In June, the two planets Uranus and Neptune are in semi-square to one another. As the great W. D. Gann noted, when this aspect occurs in the first half of the year, there is often disruption to crop growing, and very often, flooding along the Mississippi. Sugar may not be the only crop affected. Other food crops could be similarly washed out.

Of course, should there be a lack, then there will surely also be rising prices. Recall that Jupiter enters Scorpio in October 2017. Its next ingress (Sagittarius) takes place on November 8, 2018. Jupiter's move through Scorpio has coincided with increases in sugar prices in the past. Once it is known that the crop will be poor, there is every likelihood of the price increasing—especially in the weeks after the Uranus-Neptune semi-square.

2019

In 2019, both Pluto (on April 4th) and Saturn (three times: April 30th, July 4th, and September 28th) form conjunction with the lunar south Node in Cancer. Defense of realms (wars) and the uprooting of peoples as they seek sanctuary are indicated. As has been suggested above, this period could also see an escalation in the number of companies moving from one jurisdiction to another as they seek to protect their wealth.

Just how dramatic a year of change this will be should be apparent between the first New Moon of 2019—January 5th (chart opposite)—which is a solar eclipse (in the sign of Capricorn), and the lunar eclipse two weeks later on January 21st. Through this period, the reinforcement of border controls could dominate headlines.

There are several lunar-related reasons to be concerned about the first three months of the year: the January eclipses are followed by a super Moon, where the Full Moon is also at its closest to Earth, and then the Full Moon of March 21st that coincides with an Equinox. This might not be the easiest of quarters for equities, with some businesses suffering calamity as a result of weather-related chaos and catastrophe.

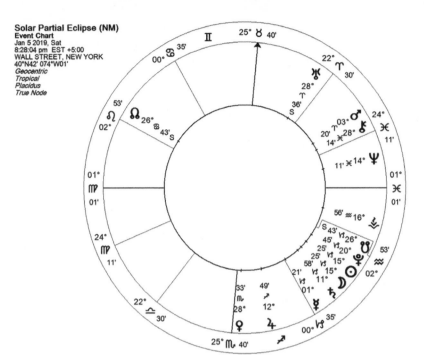

Solar Partial Eclipse (NM)
Event Chart
Jan 5 2019, Sat
8:28:04 pm EST +5:00
WALL STREET, NEW YORK
40°N42' 074°W01'
Geocentric
Tropical
Placidus
True Node

As if this were not enough, both Chiron (February 18th to Aries) and Uranus (March 6th to Taurus) make new ingress indicating changing needs and market turbulence. Though this should coincide with marked developments in design technology and robotic engineering, and so boost the values of companies working in those sectors. It is also likely to coincide with extreme pain and discontinuity for those whose products are quickly deemed redundant.

Just one degree ahead of Saturn's alignment with the lunar south Node in April, the planet opposes the highly sensitive degree of 19 Capricorn. Saturn retrogrades and then returns to this degree in September. It seems reasonable to expect downturns in all indices at these times and for the banking, lending and mortgages industries to suffer greatly. This forecast could be particularly apt if war does indeed drive people from previously safe areas.

In early September, and though invisible as it transits the other side of the Sun, Mars forms its regular conjunction with the Sun and is at its furthest point from Earth. Mars will not be observable from Earth for some weeks. It is, of course, possible that hostilities will subside as the red planet makes this conjunction, but equally likely that as it re-emerges and then moves on into Libra—where it will be at right angles to the Nodes, Saturn and Pluto, that tensions will increase once more.

It is not abnormal for the last days of October to coincide with difficulties in the marketplace. Taking into account the above mentioned Mars aspects which coincide with the Sun's passage through Scorpio, the period October 22nd to mid-November should prove very challenging.

A glimmer of hope in the form of Jupiter's conjunction with the Galactic Center in the last fortnight of November suggests there could be a quick re-bound before the end of the year. Indeed, there may be a good argument for taking any profit mid-December. The approaching Saturn-Pluto conjunction of 2020 suggests further chill financial winds.

2020–2021

It has long been thought that the planets play their own music. The successive conjunctions of, for example, the Sun and Mars, may be thought of as the occasional trumpet clarion calls of a grand symphony. Within that symphony—and not necessarily coinciding with those fanfares—heavy duty organ chords will be heard. As we have seen, between 2019 and 2021, modulation takes place as a series of relatively infrequent conjunctions occur. These planetary "chords" may well coincide with dramatic economic and political activity.

This conjunction of Jupiter and Saturn in Aquarius in December 2020 is termed a Grand Mutation. It is the first of a series of Jupiter-Saturn conjunctions to occur in Air signs. True, there was one Jupiter-Saturn conjunction in Libra in the early 1980s: a decade during which many feel that global financial management was tested as derivatives and other financial tools came to market. There is high probability that over the next two centuries, as the "Air" effect gathers momentum, that financial dealings not based on actual and tangible currencies or materials, will grow: though a real surge in these artificial dealings is most likely to come after the next Jupiter-Saturn conjunction in 2040.

In the 2020s these new style derivatives and other artificial dealings will no doubt vie with tangible currencies for supremacy. Some societies will surely find it difficult to move from hard to soft currencies.

Though it might, at first, seem obvious to suggest investing in new technologies—given that the two planets conjunct in Aquarius in 2020, it is possible to be more specific. Aquarius sectors cover all companies involved in invention, (particularly space exploration related), aviation, science, research, electrical appliances, and networking through membership in groups. Aquarius is said to pull like-minded people together—sometimes with political bias. It is also the sign said to "do things differently," and is eminently suited to crowd-funding.

We should anticipate a growth in Facebook, Linked-In, Twitter, Skype and WhatsApp-type companies: the essential difference being that rather than being "open to all" these may be targeted at specific interest groups. It seems reasonable to anticipate a surge of interest in physics and technology. These might even be areas of interest to toy manufacturers seeking to diversify.

Perhaps though the most obvious area of influence for this particular conjunction will be growth in the number of humanitarian organizations whose work will no doubt be needed, given the apparently never-ending number of refugees seeking sanctuary from conflict. The packaging of products and distribution of aid will surely exercise the talents of diplomats and envoys. Firms offering logistical support and, perhaps, knowledgeable couriers, should see demand for their services growing.

In December 2021, Jupiter leaves Aquarius and makes its Pisces ingress while the Lunar Node transits Gemini. Both are Mutable signs. With Jupiter in compassionate Pisces, this could emphasize the need to deploy aid. Such action supports the probability of NGOs assuming greater dominance on the world stage. Jupiter and the Node form a square aspect at the very beginning of 2022. Following this aspect, and taking into account that the transit of the North Node through Gemini has coincided with falling share prices in the past, we could see further decline in share values.

2022–2024

2022–2024 could be considered a period of transition. In March 2023, Pluto makes its Aquarius ingress following its long transit of Capricorn (from 2008). The probable restructuring of the banking industry ought to be nearing completion by 2024, with attention then shifting from the banking sector to industries associated with the next sign: Aquarius.

The Aquarius "financial sector" includes mutual and friendly societies and co-operative banking and insurance. It would also include companies and businesses developing computer hardware. There is a high probability that corruption in these areas will be exposed as Pluto transits Aquarius, but that the first rumblings of disquiet will be heard from 2022.

It is entirely possible too, that just as the dealings of rogue traders hit the headlines as Pluto crossed the early degrees of Capricorn in 2008–09, that similar scandals will surface as Pluto leaves this sign. It might even be that during the transitional years of 2022–23, the interplay between the banks of nations and apparent independently run financial institutions (the mutual societies and non-government agencies for example) will be exposed.

Through these years eclipses occur in the signs of Taurus and Scorpio: considered to be key "financial" signs of the zodiac. Eclipses bring the closing and opening of chapters. Focusing on the eclipses (solar and Lunar) in Scorpio and noting that both Saturn and Pluto will, albeit at different times, be at right angles to the nodal axis, it seems likely that some institutions will close their doors forever: perhaps those that came into being 90 years earlier during the Great Depression. What once appeared solid and secure may be found to be anything but.

A highly significant date is July 23, 2023 when Pluto squares the nodal axis. Both will be in very late degrees of Cardinal signs.

The Moon too will be anaretic (within a degree of changing signs), but boosted as part of a mystic rectangle formation as it sextiles the Sun and opposes Neptune, while Pluto moves to opposes the Sun at 0 Leo. That same day Venus reaches a station before turning retrograde. When the chart is set for close of trade that day in London, Neptune is within orb of the Midheaven chart. Losses are likely and could be linked to insurance and banking scandals.

Venus is then retrograde for some weeks before stationing direct on September 4th when prices ought to begin to rise.

There is however, one last major aspect to take place in 2023: Saturn's semi-square to Chiron in November. This too should coincide with an accounting scandal surfacing and mark yet another low for the financial sector.

FINAL WORDS

Future-forecasting is as much an art as a science. A little imagination is added to knowledge of developing planetary formations and understanding of the correlation between these cosmic patterns and the history of stock market movement.

While the science is logical, imagination is likely fueled less by study of the ephemeris and more by prevailing conditions. I have little doubt that were I to be making these forecasts in two years time for example, that though the dates selected would be the same, I might reach different conclusions.

This book is intended to be one of a series. To keep up to date with my thinking and future books, you are welcome to sign up for my free monthly financial newsletter at:

www.financialuniverse.co.uk.

Index

Acknowledgments

Encouragement to write this book came from many readers of my monthly "Financial Universe" letter. The incubation period was long and there were many false starts. Finally, and thanks to patient mentoring from Graham Bates, the book found form. Graham's advice and careful observations are most gratefully acknowledged.

My good friend and colleague, Priscilla Costello, introduced me to Yvonne Paglia in Florida, USA. Yvonne was enthusiastic about the book and agreed to publish it as I wanted it to be: complete with both horoscopes and technical charts. The former were prepared using Solar Fire software and the latter, using the Optuma platform. Thanks to both Priscilla and Yvonne for their confidence, and to Scott Silverman for his proofing skills.

I am grateful too to both Mathew Verdouw and Darren Hawkins at Optuma who gave unqualified support and patiently guided me through their amazing program.

Ultimately, however, it was the expertise of Jim Wasserman at Studio 31 that brought *Exploring the Financial Universe* to production stage. Jim's eagle eyes spotted errors I had missed. Thanks to him, the final presentation is everything I hoped for.

My family have put up with my ever-changing moods as I alternately got enthusiastic and then despondent about this work. I am sure that they are relieved that "Exploring" is now off my desk. I hope that they know just how very much-loved and appreciated they all are. Constantly they encourage me to be the best that I can be.

I would like to dedicate the book to my late brother, Mike Underwood—with apologies for not following his recommendations for the book's title—but in the knowledge that he would have been delighted that I finished what I started.